CW00958613

# SPANISH
## In Your Pocket

NEW
HOLLAND

# GLOBETROTTER™

First edition published in 2004
by New Holland Publishers Ltd
London • Cape Town • Sydney
• Auckland
10 9 8 7 6 5

website:
www.newhollandpublishers.com

Garfield House, 86 Edgware Road
London W2 2EA
United Kingdom

80 McKenzie Street
Cape Town 8001
South Africa

14 Aquatic Drive
Frenchs Forest, NSW 2086
Australia

218 Lake Road
Northcote, Auckland
New Zealand

Although every effort has been made
to ensure that this guide is correct at
time of going to print, the Publisher
accepts no responsibility or liability for
any loss, injury or inconvenience
incurred by readers or travellers
using this guide.

**Publishing Manager (UK):**
Simon Pooley
**Publishing Manager (SA):**
Thea Grobbelaar
**Designer:** Lellyn Creamer
**Illustrator:** Marisa Galloway
**Editor:** Thea Grobbelaar
**Translator:** José Hares
**Consultant:** Lynn Zinn
**Proofreader:** Manuel Lijó Pedro

Reproduction by Resolution, Cape Town
Printed and bound in India by
Replika Press Pvt. Ltd

**Cover photograph:** *A café in
Valencia, Spain.*

# CONTENTS

# INTRODUCTION

This PHRASE BOOK is thematically colour-coded for easy use and is organized according to the situation you're most likely to be in when you need it. The fairly comprehensive DICTIONARY section consists of two parts – English/Spanish and Spanish/English.

To make speaking Spanish easy, we encourage our readers to memorize some general PRONUNCIATION rules (*see* page 8). After you have familiarized yourself with the basic tools of the language and the rudiments of Spanish GRAMMAR (see page 14), all you need to do is turn to the appropriate section of the phrase book and find the words you need to make yourself understood. If the selection is not exactly what you're looking for, consult the dictionary for other options.

Just to get you started, here are some Spanish expressions you might have heard, read or used at some time: *adiós, por favor, gracias, hasta mañana, siesta*. Even if you are unfamiliar with these words and would rather not try to say them out loud, just remain confident, follow our easy advice and practise a little, and you will soon master useful phrases for everyday life. Speak slowly and enunciate carefully and your counterpart is likely to follow suit.

Some Spanish words, especially those ending in -ion, are pronounced differently from their English equivalents (e.g. extensión – *ex-ten-syon*), or else changed just slightly (mayonnaise – *mayonesa*), though their meanings remain clear. Nowadays many English terms are used in Spanish, especially in business, sport and leisure activities, so everyone will know what you mean when you say things like 'laptop', 'golf' and 'tennis'.

A section on HOLIDAYS AND FESTIVALS (*see* page 82) provides some background knowledge so that you know what you're celebrating and why. There's no better way to learn a language than joining in some enjoyment!

The brief section on manners, mannerisms and ETIQUETTE (*see* page 76) can help you make sense of the people around you. Make an effort to view your host country and its people tolerantly – that way you will be open to the new experience and able to enjoy it.

5

Learning a new language can be a wonderful but frightening experience. It is not the object of this book to teach you perfect Spanish, but rather to equip you with just enough knowledge for a successful holiday or business trip. Luckily you are unlikely to be criticized on your grammatical correctness when merely asking for directions. The most important thing is to make yourself understood. To this end a brief section on grammar and a guide to pronunciation have been included in this book. There is, however, no substitute for listening to native speakers.

Before you leave, it might be a good idea to familiarize yourself with the sections on Pronunciation, Grammar and Etiquette. This can easily be done en route to your destination. You will also benefit from memorizing a few important phrases before you go.

The sections of the Phrase Book are arranged by topic for quick reference. Simply go to the contents list (*see* page 3) to find the topic you need. The Dictionary section (*see* page 88) goes both ways, helping you to understand and be understood.

Abbreviations have been used in those instances where one English word could be interpreted as more than one part of speech, e.g. 'smoke' (a noun, the substance coming from a fire) and 'smoke' (a verb, what one would do with a cigarette). Here is a list of these and some other abbreviations used in this book:

| | |
|---|---|
| vb | verb |
| n | noun |
| adj | adjective |
| adv | adverb |
| prep | preposition |
| pol | polite |
| fam | familiar (informal) |
| elec | electric/al |
| med | medical |
| anat | anatomy |
| rel | religion |

The gender and number of Spanish nouns have been specified as follows:

| | |
|---|---|
| m | masculine |
| f | feminine |
| pl | plural |

Spanish is a phonetic language, so with a bit of practice you can soon read most of it. Many letters are pronounced much like the English equivalent. The English words given here contain sounds that approximate Spanish sounds.

## VOWELS
VOCALES

- **a** – like the **a** in father – *gato*
- **e** – like the **e** in let – *me*
- **i** – like the **ee** in meet – *hijo*
- **o** – like the **o** in order – *yo*
- **u** – like the **oo** in foot, but shorter – *tu*

**NB** The letter **u** following a **g** or a **q** is silent, unless marked with an umlaut – *desagüe*.

## DIPHTHONGS
DIPTONGOS

- **ai** – like the **i** in bite – *bailar*
- **ay** – like the **i** in bite – *hay*
- **au** – like the **ow** in c**ow** – *audiencia*
- **ei** – like the **ey** in th**ey** – *reina*
- **ey** – like the **ey** in th**ey** – *ley*
- **eu** – sound each vowel separately – *Europa*
- **ia** – like the **ya** in **y**ard – *enviar*

9

- **ie** – like the **ye** in **yes** – *tiene*
- **io** – like the **yo** in **yo**re – *junio*
- **iu** – like **you** – *viuda*
- **oi** – like the **oy** in **toy** – *boicot*
- **oy** – like the **oy** in **toy** – *estoy*
- **ua** – like the **wa** in **want** – *cuando*
- **uay** – like the **wi** in **wise** – *Uruguay*
- **ue** – like the **wea** in **weather** – *bueno*
- **uey** – like the **wai** in **wait** – *buey*
- **ui** – like the **wee** in **week** – *suizo*
- **uo** – like the **wo** in **woke** – *cuota*

If a vowel is marked with an accent (e.g. é, á), it indicates that this syllable is stressed.

## CONSONANTS
CONSONANTES

- **b** – see **v**
- **c** – like the **k** in **keep** – *cabeza*
- **c** – before **e** and **i**, like the **s** in **site** (used in this book) or like the **th** in **thin** – *cielo*
- **ch** – like the **ch** in **chop** – *mucho*
- **d** – between vowels or at the end of a word, it sounds like the **th** in **father** – *cada*
- **g** – before **e** and **i**, it sounds like the **ch** in lo**ch** (represented as **kh** in this book) – *gente*

- **g** – like the **g** in **g**et – *gato*
- **h** – the letter **h** is always silent – *hola*
- **j** – like the **ch** in lo**ch** (represented as **kh** in this book) – *jueves*
- **ll** – like the **y** in **y**et – *silla*
- **ñ** – like the **ny** in ca**ny**on – *niño*
- **q** – like the **c** in **c**ar – *querer*
- **r** – rolled as in Scots – *pero*
- **rr** – a lengthened rolled **r** sound – *perro*
- **s** – always pronounced like the **s** in **s**oap, never like the **s** in ea**s**y – *mesa*
- **v** – at the beginning of a word or after m or n, like the **b** in **b**ird (but less percussive) – *viento*
- **v** – in any other position, like a cross between the English **b** and **v** (with the lips barely meeting) – *mover*
- **z** – like the **th** in **th**ing – *azul*

There are variations in the pronunciation of Spanish, depending on where it is spoken, e.g. Latin America, Andalucía or the rest of Spain. The letter **z**, for example, could sound like the **th** in **th**ing, but in Latin America it would be pronounced like the **s** in **s**imple. Wherever you are, you will soon know how to pronounce the words simply by listening to the local people speaking.

Practise a few phrases in Spanish (the stressed syllables are underlined:

**Buenos días**
*bwe-nos dee-yas*
Good day

**¡Hola!**
*o-la*
Hello!

**Adiós**
*ad-yos*
Goodbye

**¿Habla inglés?**
*ab-la in-gless*
Do you speak English?

**Hable despacio, por favor**
*ab-leh des-paa-syoh, por fa-vor*
Please speak slowly

**No entiendo**
*noh ent-yen-doh*
I don't understand

**¿Cómo está usted?**
*koh-moh es-ta oos-ted*
How are you? (polite)

**¿Qué tal?**
*keh tal*
How are you? (familiar)

**Bien, gracias**
*byen, graa-syass*
Fine, thanks!

**Quiero ...**
*kyeh-roh*
I'd like ...

**¿Cómo dice?**
*ko-mo dee-seh*
Pardon?

**Por favor**
*por fa-vor*

**¡Gracias!**
*graa-syass*
Thank you!

**¡Lo siento!**
   **(¡Disculpe!)**
*loh syen-toh*
   *(dis-cool-peh)*
Sorry! Excuse me!

**¿Por dónde están**
   **los servicios?**
*por don-deh es-tahn*
   *los ser-vee-syos*
Where are the toilets?

**¿Cuándo llega el**
   **tren?**
*kwan-doh yeh-gah*
   *el trenn*
When does the train
   arrive?

**¿Dónde está?**
*don-deh es-tah*
Where is it?

**¿Puedo ...?**
*pweh-doh*
May I ...?

**ayer**
*ah-yehr*
yesterday

**hoy**
*oy*
today

**mañana**
*ma-nya-na*
tomorrow

**¿Puedo llamar por**
   **teléfono?**
*pweh-doh yah-mahr*
   *por te-leh-foh-noh*
May I use the phone?

The grammar section has deliberately been kept very brief as this is not a language course.

## PERSONAL PRONOUNS
PRONOMBRES PERSONALES

<u>Subject</u>

| | |
|---|---|
| yo | I |
| tú | you (fam) |
| usted (ud.) | you (pol) |
| él, ella | he/she |
| nosotros/as | we |
| vosotros/as | you (pl fam) |
| ustedes (uds.) | you (pl pol) |
| ellos/ellas | they |

<u>Direct Object</u>

| | |
|---|---|
| me | me |
| you | te (fam) |
| you | le (pol) |
| him | le |
| her | la |
| it | lo |
| us | nos |
| you | os (pl fam) |
| you | les (pl pol) |
| them | les |

<u>Indirect Object</u>

| | |
|---|---|
| (to) me | me |
| (to) you | te (fam) |
| (to) you | le (pol) |
| (to) him | le |
| (to) her | le |
| (to) it | le |
| (to) us | nos |
| (to) you | os (pl fam) |
| (to) you | les (pl pol) |
| (to) them | les |

## Reflexive Pronoun

| | |
|---|---|
| myself | me |
| yourself | te (fam) |
| yourself | se (pol) |
| himself | se |
| herself | se |
| itself | se |
| ourselves | nos |
| yourselves | os (pl fam) |
| yourselves | se (pl pol) |
| themselves | se |

## Possessive Pronoun

| | |
|---|---|
| mine | mío/a |
| yours | tuyo/a (fam) |
| yours | suyo/a (pol) |
| his | suyo/a, suyos/as, de él |
| hers | suyo/a, suyos/as, de ella |
| its | suyo/a, suyos/as |
| ours | nuestro/a, nuestros/as |
| yours | vuestro/a, vuestros/as (pl fam) |
| yours | suyo/a, suyos/as (pl pol) |
| theirs | suyo/a, suyos/as |

The gender of a pronoun refers to the gender of the object you are talking about, and not to your own gender. Whether you yourself are male or female, you would say the book (masculine) is mine (*el libro es mío*), or the house (feminine) is mine (*la casa es mía*).

When referring to parts of your body, the possessive pronoun is not used – you would say 'the leg' (*la pierna*) rather than 'my leg' (*mí pierna*)

## VERBS
VERBOS

All verbs in their infinitive form end in -ar, -er or -ir. Each verb has a stem or a root and an appropriate ending (be it -ar, -er or -ir). The stem of the verb is the part that precedes the ending. For example, the verb *cantar* (to sing) can be broken up as follows: *cant-* (root) and *-ar* (ending).

   The verbs that never change their stem and follow conjugation patterns are called *regulares* (about 75% of verbs), and the ones that change stem are called *irregulares* (about 25%).

Examples of REGULAR verbs, present tense:

**AMAR (to love)**
yo amO
tú amAS
él/ella/usted amA
nosotros amAMOS
vosotos amÁIS
ellos/ustedes amAN

**TEMER (to fear)**
yo temO
tú temES
él/ella/usted temE
nosotros temEMOS
vosotros temÉIS
ellos/ustedes temEN

**PARTIR (to leave)**
yo partO
tú partES
él/ella/usted partE
nosotros partIMOS
vosotros partÍS
ellos/ustedes partEN

Here are some useful IRREGULAR verbs:

**TENER (to have)**
yo tengo
tú tienes
él/ella/usted tiene
nosotros tenemos
vosotros tenéis
ellos/ustedes tienen

**QUERER (to want)**
yo quiero
tú quieres
él/ella/usted quiere
nosotros queremos
vosotros queréis
ellos/ustedes quieren

**IR (to go)**
yo voy
tú vas
él/ella/usted va
nosotros vamos
vosotros vais
ellos/ustedes van

**PODER** (can)
yo puedo
tú puedes
él/ella/usted puede
nosotros podemos
vosotros podéis
ellos/ustedes pueden

**SER** (to be)
yo soy
tú eres
él/ella/usted es
nosotros somos
vosotros sois
ellos/ustedes son

**ESTAR** (to be)
yo estoy
tú estás
él/ella/usted está

**ESTAR** (continued)
nosotros estamos,
vosotros estáis
ellos/ustedes están

**HACER** (to make/do)
yo hago
tú haces
él/ella/usted hace
nosotros hacemos
vosotros hacéis
ellos/ustedes hacen

**DECIR** (to say)
yo digo
tú dices
él/ella/usted dice
nosotros decimos
vosotros decís
ellos/ustedes dicen

## NOUNS – SUSTANTIVOS

Nouns ending in **-o** are usually masculine and nouns ending in **-a** are usually feminine. To form the plural, add **-s** if the noun ends in a vowel and **-es** if the noun ends in a consonant.

## ARTICLES – ARTÍCULOS

**Definite Article** (Artículo Definido) – the

| | | | |
|---|---|---|---|
| *el* | (masc. sing.) | *la* | (fem. sing.) |
| *los* | (masc. pl.) | *las* | (fem. pl.) |

**Examples:**

*el libro* (the book)      *la casa* (the house)

*los libros* (the books)   *las casas* (the houses)

**Indefinite Article** (Artículo Indefinido) – a, some

| | | | |
|---|---|---|---|
| *un* | (masc. sing.) | *una* | (fem. sing.) |
| *unos* | (masc. pl.) | *unas* | (fem. pl.) |

**Examples:**

*un perro* (a dog)          *una planta* (a plant)

*unos perros* (some dogs)   *unas plantas*
                            (some plants)

## ADJECTIVES – ADJETIVOS

Adjectives usually follow the nouns they qualify
(*un libro nuevo* – a new book). Most adjectives
have a masculine and a feminine form ( red –
(*rojo/roja*) as well as a singular and plural form
(red – *rojos/rojas*). All adjectives agree in gender and number with the nouns they qualify.
Adjectives not ending in -o or -a do not change

# GRAMÁTICA

into the masculine or feminine form, but do change to form plurals (*la casa grande* – the big house; *las casas grandes* – the big houses).

## PUNCTUATION
PUNTUACIÓN

You may have noticed the upside-down questions marks and exclamation marks used on page 12. In Spanish, a question is introduced by such an upside-down question mark, and concluded with a 'right-way-up' question mark as we know it in English. The same is true of the exclamation mark.

## WORD ORDER
ORDEN DE LAS PALABRAS

Spanish word order will probably seem strange to English ears. The adjective usually comes after the noun it modifies (see page 20), but quantifying adjectives usually precede the noun (many books – *muchos libros*). The adjective also precedes the noun if you want to emphasize the adjective rather than the noun.

A question usually has exactly the same word order as a statement, but is distinguished from a statement by the two question marks.

# LOS BÁSICOS

## NUMBERS
NÚMEROS

| | |
|---|---|
| 0 | cero (*seh*-roh) |
| 1 | uno (*oo*-noh) |
| 2 | dos (*doss*) |
| 3 | tres (*tress*) |
| 4 | cuatro (*kwat*-roh) |
| 5 | cinco (*seeng*-koh) |
| 6 | seis (*sayss*) |
| 7 | siete (*s'yet*-teh) |
| 8 | ocho (*ot*-choh) |
| 9 | nueve (*nweh*-veh) |
| 10 | diez (*d'yess*) |
| 11 | once (*on*-seh) |
| 12 | doce (*doh*-seh) |
| 13 | trece (*treh*-seh) |
| 14 | catorce (kah-*torr*-seh) |
| 15 | quince (*keen*-seh) |
| 16 | dieciséis (d'yes-ee-*sayss*) |
| 17 | diecisiete (d'yes-ee-*s'yet*-teh) |
| 18 | dieciocho (d'yes-ee-*ot*-choh) |
| 19 | diecinueve (d'yes-ee-*nweh*-veh) |
| 20 | veinte (*bayn*-teh) |
| 21 | veintiuno (*bayn*-tee-*oo*-noh) |

| | |
|---|---|
| 22 | veintidós (bayn-tee-*doss*) |
| 30 | treinta (*trayn*-ta) |
| 31 | treinta y uno (*trayn*-ta-ee-*oo*-noh) |
| 40 | cuarenta (kwa-*ren*-ta) |
| 50 | cincuenta (seeng-*kwen*-ta) |
| 60 | sesenta (seh-*sen*-ta) |
| 70 | setenta (seh-*ten*-ta) |
| 80 | ochenta (otch-*en*-ta) |
| 90 | noventa (noh-*ven*-ta) |
| 100 | cien (*s'yen*) |
| 101 | ciento uno (*s'yen*-toh-*oo*-noh) |
| 120 | ciento viente (*s'yen*-toh-*bayn*-teh) |
| 200 | doscientos (doss-*s'yen*-toss) |
| 500 | quinientos (keen-*yen*-toss) |
| 1000 | mil (*meel*) |
| 1 million | un millón (oon mee-*yon*) |
| 1 billion | un billón (oon bee-*yon*) |

23

| **DAYS** DÍAS | **MONTHS** MESES |
|---|---|

**Monday**
lunes (*loo*-ness)

**Tuesday**
martes (*marr*-tess)

**Wednesday**
miércoles
(*m'yehr*-koh-less)

**Thursday**
jueves (*khweh*-vess)

**Friday**
viernes (*b'yer*-ness)

**Saturday**
sábado (*sabba*-doh)

**Sunday**
domingo
(doh-*meeng*-goh)

**weekdays**
días de semana (*dee*-yass deh seh-*ma*-na)

**weekends**
fines de semana (*fee*-ness deh seh-*ma*-na)

**public holidays**
feriados (ferr-*ya*-doss)

**January**
enero (eh-*neh*-roh)

**February**
febrero (feb-*reh*-roh)

**March**
marzo (*marr*-soh)

**April**
abril (ab-*reel*)

**May**
mayo (*ma*-yoh)

**June**
junio (*khoon*-yoh)

**July**
julio (*khool*-yoh)

**August**
agosto (a*goss*-toh)

**September**
setiembre (set-*yem*-breh)

**October**
octubre (ok-*too*-breh)

**November**
noviembre
(nov-*yem*-breh)

24

**December**
diciembre
*(dees-yem-breh)*

| TIME |
| LA HORA |

**in the morning**
por la mañana
*(porr la man-ya-na)*

**in the afternoon**
por la tarde
*(porr la tarr-deh)*

**in the evening**
por la noche
*(por la notche)*

**What is the time?**
¿Qué hora es?
*(keh oh-ra ess)*

◆ **it's one o'clock**
◆ es la una *(ess la oo-na)*

◆ **it's quarter to three**
◆ son las tres menos cuarto *(son lass tress mennos kwarr-toh)*

◆ **it's half past two**
◆ son las dos y media *(son lass doss ee med-ya)*

◆ **twenty past two**
◆ son las dos y veinte *(son lass doss ee bayn-teh)*

◆ **early**
◆ temprano *(tem-pra-noh)*

◆ **late**
◆ tarde *(tarr-deh)*

**at 10 a.m. (10:00)**
a las diez de la mañana
*(allas d'yess della man-ya-na)*

**at 5 p.m. (17:00)**
a las cinco de la tarde
*(allas seeng-koh della tarr-deh)*

**at 9 p.m. (21:00)**
a las nueve de la noche
*(allas nweh-veh della notcheh)*

**day after tomorrow**
pasado mañana
*(pa-saa-doh man-ya-na)*

**day before yesterday**
anteayer *(anteh-a-yerr)*

**this morning**
esta mañana
*(ess-ta man-ya-na)*

**yesterday evening**
ayer por la noche/tarde
*(a-yerr porr la notcheh/*
*tarr-deh)*

**tomorrow morning**
mañana por la mañana
*(man-ya-na porr la*
*man-ya-na)*

**last night**
anoche *(a-notcheh)*

**this week**
esta semana
*(ess-ta seh-ma-na)*

**next week**
la semana próxima *(la*
*seh-ma-na prok-see-ma)*

**now**
ahora *(a-oh-ra)*

**What is today's**
**date?**
¿A cuantos estamos hoy?
*(a kwan-tos ess-ta-moss*
*oy)*
¿Qué día es hoy?
*(keh dee-ya ess oy)*

**It's 4 June**
Es el cuatro de junio
*(ess ell kwat-roh de*
*khoon-yoh)*

---

| GREETINGS |
|:---:|
| SALUDOS |

**Good morning**
Buenos días
*(bwennoss dee-yass)*

**Good afternoon**
Buenas tardes
*(bwennass tarr-dess)*

**Good evening**
Buenas tardes/noches
*(bwennass tarr-dess/*
*notchess)*

**Good night**
Buenas noches
*(bwennass notchess)*

**Hello**
Hola *(Olla)*

**Goodbye**
Adiós *(ad-yoss)*

**Cheerio**
Chau *(chow)*

**See you soon**
Hasta pronto
*(ass-ta pron-toh)*

**See you later**
Hasta luego
*(ass-ta lwe-goh)*

**Have a good time**
Que te diviertas/que la
pases bien *(keh teh
deev-yehr-tass/
keh la passess byen)*

**I have to go now**
Debo irme ahora *(deb-
boh eer-meh a-oh-ra)*

**It was very nice**
Fue muy agradable *(fweh
mooee agra-da-bleh)*

**My name is ...**
Mi nombre es ...
*(mee nom-breh ess ...)*

**What is your name?**
¿Cómo se llama? (pol)
*(kom-moh seh yaa-ma)*
¿Cómo te llamas? (fam)
*(kom-moh teh yaa-mass)*

**Pleased to meet you!**
¡Mucho gusto!
*(moo-choh goos-toh)*

**How are you?**
¿Cómo está? (pol)
*(kom-moh ess-ta)*
¿Que tal? (fam) *(keh tal)*

**Fine, thanks. And you?**
Bien, gracias. ¿Y usted?
(pol)
*(byen graas-yass, ee
oos-ted)*

## GENERAL
### GENERALES

**Do you speak English?**
¿Hablas inglés?
*(ab-las eeng-gless)*

**I don't understand**
No comprendo/ no
entiendo *(noh kom-pren-
doh/noh ent-yen-doh)*

**Please speak slowly**
Por favor, habla despacio
*(por fa-vor, ab-la
des-pa-s'yoh)*

**Please repeat that**
Por favor, repite eso
*(por fa-vor, reh-pee-teh
essoh)*

**Please write it down**
Por favor, escríbelo *(por
fa-vor, es-cree-beh-loh)*

**Excuse me please**
Discúlpame/perdóname
*(dees-cool-pa-meh/
per-donna-meh)*

**Could you help me?**
¿Me puedes ayudar?
*(meh pweh-dess
a-yoo-darr)*

27

**Could you do me a favour?**
¿Puedes hacerme un favor? *(pweh-dess a-serr-meh oon fa-vor)*

**Can you show me?**
¿Puedes mostrarme? *(pweh-dess moss-trarr-meh)*

**how?**
¿cómo? *(kom-moh)*

**where?**
¿dónde? *(donn-deh)*

**when?**
¿cuándo? *(kwan-doh)*

**who?**
¿quién? *(k'yen)*

**why?**
¿por qué? *(porr keh)*

**which?**
¿cuál? *(kwal)*

**I need ...**
necesito ...
*(ne-seh-see-toh ...)*

**yes**
sí *(see)*

**no**
no *(noh)*

---

**FORMS & SIGNS**
IMPRESOS & SIGNOS

**Please complete in block letters**
Rellene con mayúsculas de imprenta, por favor *(reh-yen-neh con ma-yoos-cool-las deh eem-pren-ta, por fa-vor)*

**Surname**
Apellido *(appeh-yee-doh)*

**First names**
Nombres *(nom-bress)*

**Date of birth**
Fecha de nacimiento *(fetcha deh nasee-m'yen-toh)*

**Place of birth**
Lugar de nacimiento *(loo-garr deh nasee-m'yen-toh)*

**Occupation**
Profesión *(proh-fes-s'yon)*

**Nationality**
Nacionalidad *(na-s'yoh-nalli-dad)*

**Address**
Dirección *(dee-rec-s'yon)*

**Date of arrival**
Fecha de llegada *(fetcha deh yeg-ga-da)*

**Date of departure**
Fecha de partida *(fetcha deh parr-tee-dah)*

**Passport number**
Número de pasaporte *(noo-meh-roh deh passa-por-teh)*

**I.D. number**
Número de documento de identidad *(noo-meh-roh deh dok-oo-men-toh deh ee-dentee-dad)*

**Issued at**
Expedido en *(expeh-dee-doh en)*

**Engaged, Vacant**
Ocupado, Libre *(okkoo-pa-doh, lee-breh)*

**No trespassing**
No pasar *(noh pas-sarr)*

**Out of order**
No funciona *(noh foon-s'yoh-na)*

**Please don't disturb**
Por favor, no moleste *(por fa-vor, noh moh-less-teh)*

**Push, Pull**
Empuje, Tire *(em-poo-kheh, tee-reh)*

**Adults and children**
Adultos y niños *(a-dool-toss ee neen-yoss)*

**Lift/Elevator**
Ascensor/Elevador *(as-senn-sorr/ele-va-dorr)*

**Escalator**
Escalera mecánica *(es-ca-leh-ra meh-ka-nee-ka)*

**Wet paint**
Pintura fresca *(peen-too-ra fress-ka)*

**Open, Closed**
Abierto, Cerrado *(ab'yer-toh, ser-ra-doh)*

**Till/Cash Desk**
Caja *(ka-kha)*

**Opening hours**
Horario de trabajo *(or-raar-yoh deh tra-ba-khoh)*

**Self-service**
Autoservicio *(aoo-toh-serr-vee-s'yoh)*

**Waiting Room**
Sala de espera *(sa-la deh ess-peh-rah)*

## BUS/TRAM STOP
PARADA DE AUTOBÚS/TRANVÍA

### Where is the bus/tram stop?
¿Dónde está la parada de autobús/tranvía?
(*Donn*-deh ess-*ta* la pa-*ra*-da deh aoo-toh-*booss*/tram-*bee*-ya)

### Which bus do I take?
¿Cuál autobús debo tomar? (Kwal aoo-toh-*booss* debboh toh-*marr*)

### How often do the buses go?
¿Con qué frecuencia pasan los buses? (Kon *keh* freh-*kwens*-ya *pas*-san loss *booss*-ess)

### When is the last bus?
¿A qué hora pasa el ultimo autobús? (A keh *oh*-ra *passa* ell *ool*-tee-moh aoo-toh-*booss*)

### Which ticket must I buy?
¿Cuál billete debo comprar? (Kwal bee-*yet*-teh *debboh* kom-*prarr*)

### Where must I go?
¿Dónde debo ir?
(*Donn*-deh *debboh* eer)

### I want to go to ....
Quiero ir a…
(K'*yeh*-roh eer a …)

### What is the fare to...?
¿Cuánto cuesta a …?
(*Kwan*-toh kwess-ta a …)

### When is the next bus?
¿En cuánto tiempo llegará el próximo Autobús?
(En *kwan*-toh t'*yem*-poh yegga-*ra* ell *prok*-see-moh aoo-toh-*booss*)

## UNDERGROUND/ SUBWAY/METRO
METRO/ SUBTERRÁNEO

### entrance, exit
entrada, salida
(en-*tra*-da, sa-*lee*-da)

### inner zone, outer zone
zona interna, zona externa
(*soh*-na een-*terr*-na, *soh*-na ex-*terr*-na)

**Where is the under-ground/subway station?**
¿Dónde está la estación de metro? (*Donn*-deh ess-*ta* la es-ta-s'*yon* deh *met*-roh)

**Do you have a map for the metro?**
¿Tiene un mapa para el metro? (*T'yen*-neh oon *mappa parra* ell *met*-roh)

**I want to go to ....**
Quiero ir a...
(*K'yeh*-roh eer a ...)

**Can you give me change?**
¿Puede cambiarme/darme cambio? (*Pweh*-deh kam-b'*yarr*-meh/*darr*-meh *kam*-b'yoh)

**Which ticket must I buy?**
¿Cuál billete debo comprar? (Kwal bee-*yet*-teh *debboh* kom-*prarr*)

**When is the next train?**
¿En cuánto tiempo llegará el próximo tren? (En *kwan*-toh t'*yem*-poh yegga-*ra* ell *prok*-see-moh *trenn*)

---

**TRAIN/RAILWAY**
TREN/FERROCARRIL

**Where is the railway station?**
¿Dónde está la estación de tren? (*Donn*-deh ess-*ta* la es-ta-s'*yon* deh *trenn*)

**departure**
salidas (sa-*lee*-dass)

**arrival**
llegadas (yeg-*ga*-dass)

**Which platform?**
¿Cuál plataforma?
(*Kwal* platta-*for*-ma)

**Do you have a timetable?**
¿Tiene un horario? (*T'yen*-neh oon or-*raar*-yoh)

**A ... ticket please**
Un billete ... por favor
(*Oon* bee-*yet*-teh ... por fa-*vor*)

◆ **single**
◆ ida (*ee*-da)

◆ **return**
◆ ida y vuelta
(*ee*-da ee *bwel*-ta)

32

- **child's**
- infantil *(een-fan-teel)*

- **first class**
- primera clase
  *(pree-meh-ra kla-seh)*

- **second class**
- segunda clase
  *(seh-goon-da kla-seh)*

- **smoking**
- fumador *(foo-ma-dorr)*

- **non-smoking**
- no fumador *(noh
  foo-ma-dorr)*

**Do I have to pay a
supplement?**
¿Debo pagar exceso?
*(Debboh pa-garr
ex-sessoh)*

**Is my ticket valid on
this train?**
¿Mi billete es válido en
este tren? *(Mee bee-yet-
teh ess ba-lee-doh en
ess-teh trenn)*

**Where do I have to
get off?**
¿Dónde debo bajarme?
*(Donn-deh debboh
ba-khar-meh)*

**I want to book ...**
Quiero reservar ...
*(K'yeh-roh reh-ser-varr ...)*

- **a seat**
- un asiento
  *(oon ass-yen-toh)*

- **a couchette**
- un coche cama
  *(oon kotcheh ca-ma)*

**Is this seat free?**
¿Este asiento está
ocupado? *(Ess-teh
ass-yen-toh ess-ta
okkoo-pa-doh)*

**That is my seat**
Ese es mi asiento
*(Es-seh ess mee
ass-yen-toh)*

**May I open (close)
the window?**
¿Puedo abrir (cerrar) la
ventana? *(Pweh-doh
ab-reer [ser-rarr] la
ben-ta-na)*

**Where is the
restaurant car?**
¿Dónde está el coche
comedor? *(Donn-deh
ess-ta ell kotcheh
kommeh-dorr)*

**Is there a sleeper?**
¿Hay una coche cama?
*(Aee oo-na kotcheh ca-ma)*

**EC – Eurocity**
International express,
supplement payable

**IC – Intercity**
Luxury international
express, supplement
payable

**stationmaster**
jefe de estación *(khef-feh
deh ess-ta-s'yon)*

---

**BOATS**
BARCOS

---

**cruise**
crucero *(kroo-seh-roh)*

**Can we hire a boat?**
¿Podemos alquilar un
barco/bote? *(Poh-deh-
moss al-kee-larr oon
barr-koh/boh-teh)*

**How much is a
round trip?**
¿Cuánto cuesta un viaje
de ida y vuelta?
*(Kwan-toh kwes-ta oon
b'ya-kheh deh ee-da ee
bwel-ta)*

**one ticket**
un billete
*(oon bee-yet-teh)*

**two tickets**
dos billetes
*(doss bee-yet-tess)*

**Can we eat on
board?**
¿Se puede comer a
bordo? *(Seh pweh-deh
ko-merr a borr-doh)*

**When is the last
boat?**
¿A qué hora sale el último
barco? *(A keh oh-ra sa-leh
ell ool-tee-moh barr-koh)*

**When is the next
ferry?**
¿A qué hora sale la
próxima barca/
transbordador?
*(A keh oh-ra sa-leh la
prok-see-ma barr-ka/
trans-borda-dorr)*

**How long does the
crossing take?**
¿Cuánto tarda el cruce?
*(Kwan-toh tarr-da ell
kroo-seh)*

**Is the sea rough?**
¿El mar está bravo?
*(Ell marr ess-ta bra-voh)*

## TAXI
TAXI

**Please order me a taxi**
Por favor, llame un taxi *(Por fa-vor, ya-meh oon taxi)*

**Where can I get a taxi?**
¿Dónde puedo coger/tomar un taxi?
*(Donn-deh pweh-doh ko-kherr/toh-marr oon taxi)*

**To this address, please**
A esta dirección, por favor *(A ess-ta dee-reks-s'yon, por fa-vor)*

**How much is it to the centre?**
¿Cuánto cuesta al centro de la ciudad?*(Kwan-toh kwess-ta al sen-troh della see-oo-dad)*

**To the airport, please**
Al aeropuerto, por favor *(Al a-ehroh-pwerr-toh, por fa-vor)*

**To the station, please**
A la estación, por favor *(Alla es-ta-s'yon por fa-vor)*

**Keep the change**
Quédese con el cambio *(Keh-deh-seh kon ell kam-b'yoh)*

**I need a receipt**
Necesito un recibo *(Ne-seh-see-toh oon reh-see-boh*

## AIRPORT
AEROPUERTO

**arrival**
llegadas *(yeg-ga-dass)*

**departure**
salidas *(sa-lee-dass)*

**flight number**
número de vuelo *(noo-meh-roh deh bweh-loh)*

**delay**
retraso *(re-tra-soh)*

**check-in**
facturación de equipages *(fak-too-ra-s'yon deh ekkee-pa-khess)*

**hand luggage**
equipaje de mano *(ekkee-pa-khe deh ma-noh)*

**boarding card**
tarjeta de embarque
(tarr-<u>kheh</u>-ta deh
em-<u>barr</u>-keh)

**gate**
puerta (p<u>werr</u>-ta)

**valid, invalid**
válido, inválido (<u>ba</u>-lee-
doh, eem-<u>ba</u>-lee-doh)

**baggage/luggage
claim**
recolección de equipajes
(rekko-lek-s'<u>yon</u> deh
ekkee-<u>pa</u>-khess)

**lost property office**
oficina de objetos
perdidos (offee-<u>see</u>-na
deh ob-<u>khe</u>-toss perr-
<u>dee</u>-doss)

**Where do I get the
bus to the centre?**
¿Dónde cojo/tomo el
autobús a la ciudad?
(<u>Donn</u>-deh <u>koh</u>-khoh/
<u>toh</u>-moh ell aoo-toh-
<u>booss</u> alla see-oo-<u>dad</u>)

**Where do I check in
for ...?**
¿Dónde está el mostrador
de ...? (<u>Donn</u>-deh ess-<u>ta</u>
ell moss-tra-<u>dorr</u> deh ...)

**An aisle/window
seat, please**
Un asiento en pasillo/
ventanilla, por favor
(Oon ass-<u>yen</u>-toh en
pa-<u>see</u>-yoh/benta-<u>nee</u>-ya,
por fa-<u>vor</u>)

**Where is the gate for
the flight to ....?**
¿Dónde está la puerta
de embarque para el
vuelo ...? (<u>Donn</u>-deh
ess-<u>ta</u> la p<u>werr</u>-ta deh
em-<u>barr</u>-keh parra ell
<u>bweh</u>-loh ...)

**I have nothing to
declare**
Nada que declarar
(<u>Na</u>-da keh dekla-<u>rarr</u>)

**It's for my own
personal use**
Es de uso personal (Ess
deh <u>oo</u>-soh perr-soh-<u>nal</u>)

**The flight has been
cancelled**
El vuelo ha sido cancelado
(Ell <u>bweh</u>-loh a <u>see</u>-doh
kan-seh-<u>la</u>-doh)

**The flight has been
delayed**
El vuelo ha sido demorado
(Ell <u>bweh</u>-loh a <u>see</u>-doh
demoh-<u>ra</u>-doh)

## ROAD TRAVEL/ CAR HIRE
VIAJE EN CARRETERA/ ALQUILER DE VEHÍCULOS

### Have you got a road map?
¿Tiene un mapa carretero? *(T'yen-neh oon mappa karreh-teh-roh)*

### How many kilometres is it to ...?
¿Cuántos kilómetros hay a ...? *(Kwan-toss kee-lommeh-tross aee a ...)*

### Where is the nearest garage?
¿Dónde está el garaje más cercano? *(Donn-deh ess-ta ell ga-ra-kheh mahss ser-ka-noh)*

### Fill it up, please
Llene el tanque, por favor *(Yen-neh ell tan-keh, por fa-vor)*

### Please check the oil, water, battery, tyres
Por favor, controle el aceite, el agua, la batería, los neumáticos *(Por fa-vor, kon-troh-leh ell asay-teh, ell agwa, la ba-teh-ree-ya, loss neoo-ma-tee-koss)*

### I'd like to hire a car
Quiero alquilar un coche *(K'yeh-roh al-kee-larr oon kotcheh)*

### How much does it cost per day/week?
¿Cuánto cuesta por día/ semana? *(Kwan-toh kwess-ta porr dee-ya/ seh-ma-na)*

### What do you charge per kilometre?
¿Cuánto cobran por kilómetro? *(Kwan-toh kob-ran porr kee-lommeh-troh)*

### Is mileage unlimited?
¿El millaje es ilimitado? *(Ell mee-ya-kheh ess ee-leemee-ta-doh)*

### Where can I pick up the car?
¿Dónde recojo el coche? *(Donn-deh reh-koh-khoh ell kotcheh)*

### Where can I leave the car?
¿Dónde puedo dejar el coche? *(Donn-deh pweh-doh deh-kharr ell kotcheh)*

**garage**
garaje/estación de servicio (ga-_ra_-kheh/ ess-ta-s'_yon_ deh serr-_vees_-yo)

**headlight**
faro (_fa_-roh)

**windscreen**
parabrisas (parra-_bree_-sass)

**indicator**
intermitente (een-termee-_ten_-teh)

**What is the speed limit?**
¿Cuál es el límite de velocidad? (Kwal ess ell _lee_-mee-teh deh beh-loh-see-_dad_)

**The keys are locked in the car**
Las llaves están dentro del coche cerrado (Lass _ya_-vess ess-_tann_ _den_-troh dell _kotcheh_ ser-_ra_-doh)

**The engine is overheating**
El motor está recalentado (Ell moh-_torr_ ess-_ta_ reh-kallen-_ta_-doh)

**Have you got ...?**
Tiene ...? (T'_yen_-neh ...)

♦ **a towing rope**
♦ una cuerda de remolque (oona _kwerr_-da deh reh-_moll_-keh)

♦ **a spanner**
♦ una llave de tuercas (oona _ya_-veh deh _twerr_-kass)

♦ **a screwdriver**
♦ un destornillador (oon dess-tornee-ya-_dorr_)

> **ROAD SIGNS**
> SEÑALES DE TRÁFICO

**No through road**
No pasar (Noh pas-_sarr_)

**one-way street**
calle de una sola mano (_ka_-yeh deh oona _solla_ _ma_-noh)

**entrance**
entrada (en-_tra_-da)

**exit**
salida (sa-_lee_-da)

**danger**
peligro (peh-_lee_-groh)

**pedestrians**
peatones
*(peh-ya-<u>toh</u>-ness)*

**Keep entrance clear**
No bloquear la entrada
*(Noh bloh-keh-<u>yarr</u> la
en-<u>tra</u>-da)*

**Residents only**
Sólo para residentes
*(<u>Solloh</u> parra reh-see-
<u>den</u>-tess)*

**speed limit**
límite de velocidad
*(lee-mee-teh deh
beh-loh-see-<u>dad</u>)*

**stop**
pare *(<u>pa</u>-reh)*

**No entry**
Prohibida la entrada *(Pro-
ee-<u>bee</u>-da la en-<u>tra</u>-da)*

**roundabout**
rotonda *(roh-<u>ton</u>-da)*

**Insert coins**
Ponga cambio/monedas
*(<u>Pong</u>-ga <u>kam</u>-b'yoh/
moh-<u>neh</u>-dass)*

**No Parking**
Prohibido estacionar
*(Pro-ee-<u>bee</u>-doh
es-ta-s'yoh-<u>narr</u>*

**parking garage**
garaje de estacionamiento
*(ga-<u>ra</u>-kheh deh ess-ta-
s'yon-na-m'<u>yen</u>-toh)*

**supervised car park**
estacionamiento
controlado *(ess-ta-s'yon-
na-m'<u>yen</u>-toh kon-troh-
<u>la</u>-doh)*

**No right turn**
Prohibido girar a la
derecha *(pro-ee-<u>bee</u>-doh
khee-<u>rarr</u> alla deh-<u>ret</u>cha)*

**cul de sac**
calle sin salida *(<u>ka</u>-yeh
seen sa-<u>lee</u>-da)*

**roadworks**
trabajos camineros
*(tra-<u>ba</u>-khoss kamee-
<u>neh</u>-ross)*

**detour**
desvío *(dess-<u>vee</u>-oh)*

**Caution**
Cuidado *(Kwee-<u>da</u>-doh)*

**uneven surface**
calzada irregular *(kal-<u>sa</u>-da
ee-reh-goo-<u>larr</u>)*

**toll**
peaje *(peh-<u>a</u>-kheh)*

### ACCOMMODATION
ALOJAMIENTO

**bed & breakfast**
pensión *(pen-s'yon)*

**vacancies**
habitación libre *(abbee-ta-s'yon lee-breh)*

**Have you a room ...?**
¿Tiene una habitación ...?
*(T'yenn-neh oona abbee-ta-s'yon)*

◆ **for tonight**
◆ para esta noche
  *(parra ess-ta notcheh)*

◆ **with breakfast**
◆ con desayuno *(kon dessa-yoo-noh)*

◆ **with bath**
◆ con baño *(kon banyo)*

◆ **with shower**
◆ con ducha *(kon dootcha)*

◆ **a single room**
◆ habitación single/para una persona *(abbee-ta-s'yon single/parra oona per-soh-na)*

◆ **a double room**
◆ habitación doble
  *(abbee-ta-s'yon dob-bleh)*

◆ **a family room**
◆ habitación familiar
  *(abbee-ta-s'yon fa-meel-yar)*

**How much is the room ...?**
¿Cuánto cuesta la habitación ...?
*(Kwan-toh kwess-ta la abbee-ta-s'yon)*

◆ **per day/week**
◆ por día/semana *(por dee-ya/se-ma-na)*

**Have you got anything cheaper/better?**
¿Hay algo mejor/más barato? *(Aee al-goh meh-khorr/mahss ba-ra-toh)*

**May I see the room?**
¿Puedo ver la habitación? *(Pweh-doh berr la abbee-ta-s'yon)*

**Do you have a cot?**
¿Tiene una cuna?
*(T'yenn-neh oona koo-na)*

## What time is breakfast/dinner?
¿A qué hora es el desayuno/la cena? (*A keh oh-ra ess ell dessa-yoo-noh/la seh-na*)

## room service
el servicio de cuarto/habitaciones (*ell serr-vee-s'yoh deh kwarr-toh/abbee-ta-s'yon-ness*)

## Please bring ...
Por favor trae/traiga ... (*Por fa-vor tra-eh/traee-ga*)

◆ **toilet paper**
 ◆ papel higiénico (*pa-pell ee-khee-en-ee-koh*)

◆ **clean towels**
 ◆ toallas limpias (*toh-ay-yas leem-p'yass*)

## Please clean the bath
Por favor limpia la bañera (*Por fa-vor leem-p'ya la ban-yeh-ra*)

## Please put fresh sheets on the bed
Por favor, cambia las sábanas (*Por fa-vor, kam-b'ya lass sa-ba-nass*)

## Please don't touch ...
Por favor, no toques ... (*Por fa-vor, noh tok-kess*)

◆ **my briefcase**
 ◆ mi maletín (*mee ma-leh-teen*)

◆ **my laptop**
 ◆ mi ordenador/computador portátil (*mee or-deh-na-dorr/kom-poo-ta-dorr porr-ta-teel*)

## My ... doesn't work
Mi ... no funciona (*Mee ... noh foon-s'yoh-na*)

◆ **toilet**
 ◆ inodoro/lavabo (*eeno-doh-roh/la-va-boh*

◆ **bedside lamp**
 ◆ lámpara (*lam-pa-ra*)

◆ **air conditioning**
 ◆ aire acondicionado (*aee-reh akon-dee-s'yoh-na-doh*

## There is no hot water
No hay agua caliente (*Noh aee agwa kallee-yen-teh*)

## RECEPTION
RECEPCIÓN

**Are there any messages for me?**
¿Hay algún mensaje para mí? (*Aee al-<u>goon</u> men-<u>sa</u>-kheh parra <u>mee</u>*)

**Has anyone asked for me?**
¿Alguien ha preguntado por mí? (*<u>Al</u>-ghee-en a pre-goon-<u>ta</u>-doh porr <u>mee</u>*)

**Can I leave a message for someone?**
¿Puedo dejar un mensaje para alguien? (*<u>Pweh</u>-doh deh-<u>khar</u> oon men-<u>sa</u>-kheh parra <u>al</u>-ghee-en*)

**Is there a laundry service?**
¿Hay servicio de lavandería? (*<u>Aee</u> serr-<u>vee</u>-s'yoh de la-van-deh-<u>ree</u>-ya*)

**I need a wake-up call at 7 o'clock**
¿Puedes despertarme a las 7 en punto? (*<u>Pweh</u>-dess des-per-<u>tarr</u>-meh a lass s'<u>yet</u>-teh en <u>poon</u>-toh*)

**What number must I dial for room service?**
¿Cuál es el número de servicio de cuarto? (*<u>Kwal</u> ess ell <u>noo</u>-meh-roh deh serr-<u>vee</u>-s'yoh deh <u>kwarr</u>-toh*)

**Where is the lift/ elevator?**
¿Dónde está el ascensor? (*<u>Donn</u>-deh ess-<u>ta</u> ell as-sen-<u>sorr</u>*)

**Do you arrange tours?**
¿Organiza los viajes? (*Orr-ga-<u>nee</u>-sa loss b'<u>ya</u>-khess*)

**Please prepare the bill**
Por favor, prepara la cuenta (*Por fa-<u>vor</u>, preh-<u>parr</u>a la <u>kwen</u>-ta*)

**There is a mistake in this bill**
Hay un error en esta cuenta (*<u>Aee</u> oon err<u>or</u> en ess-ta <u>kwen</u>-ta*)

**I'm leaving tomorrow**
Salgo mañana (*<u>Sall</u>-goh man-<u>ya</u>-na*)

**SELF-CATERING**
ALOJAMIENTO CON
COCINA PROPIA

**Have you any vacancies?**
¿Hay lugar? *(Aee loo-garr)*

**How much is it per night/week?**
¿Cuánto cuesta por noche/semana?
*(Kwan-toh kwess-ta porr notcheh)*

**How big is it?**
¿Cuál es el tamaño?
*(Kwal ess ell ta-man-yoh)*

**Do you allow children?**
¿Se permiten niños? *(Seh per-mee-ten neen-yoss)*

**Please, show me how ... works**
Por favor, enséñame cómo ... funciona *(Por fa-vor, en-sen-ya-meh kom-moh ... foon s'yoh-na)*

♦ **the cooker/stove/ oven**
♦ la cocina/horno
*(la koh-see-na/orr-noh)*

♦ **the washing machine**
♦ la lavadora
*(la lava-doh-ra)*

♦ **the dryer**
♦ la secadora
*(la se-ka-doh-ra)*

♦ **the hair-dryer**
♦ el secador de pelo
*(ell se-ka-dorr deh peh-loh)*

♦ **the heater**
♦ el calefactor
*(ell ka-leh-fak-torr)*

♦ **the water heater**
♦ el calentador para agua
*(ell ka-lenta-dorr parra agwa)*

**Where is/are ...?**
¿Dónde está/están ...?
*(Donn-deh ess-ta/ ess-tan ...)*

♦ **the keys**
♦ las llaves *(lass ya-vess)*

♦ **the switch**
♦ el interruptor
*(ell een-ter-roop-torr)*

♦ **the fuses**
♦ los fusibles
*(loss foo-see-bless)*

**Is there ...?**
¿Hay ...? (*Aee ...*)

- **a cot**
- una cuna? (*oona koo-na*)

- **a high chair**
- una silla alta para niños
  (*oona see-ya alta parra
  neen-yoss*)

- **a safe**
- una caja fuerte (*oona
  ka-kha fwerr-teh*)

**We need more ...**
necesitamos más ... (*ne-
seh-see-ta-moss mahss*)

- **cutlery**
- cubertería
  (*koo-ber-teh-ree-ya*)

- **crockery**
- vajilla (*ba-khee-ya*)

- **sheets**
- sábanas (*sa-ba-nass*)

- **blankets**
- cobertores
  (*kobber-toh-ress*)

- **pillows**
- almohadas
  (*al-moh-aa-dass*)

**Is there ... in the
vicinity?**
¿Hay ... en el barrio?
(*Aee ... en ell barr-yo*)

- **a shop**
- una tienda
  (*oona t'yen-da*)

- **a restaurant**
- un restaurante (*oon
  resta-oo-ran-teh*)

- **a bus/tram**
- un autobús/tranvía
  (*oon aoo-toh-booss/
  tram-bee-ya*)

**We'd like to stay for
three nights/a week**
Nos gustaría quedarnos
por tres noches/una
semana (*Nos goos-ta-
ree-ya keh-darr-nos porr
tress notchess/oona
seh-ma-na*)

**I have locked
myself out**
No puedo entrar (*No
pweh-doh en-trar*)

**The window won't
open/close**
La ventana no abre/cierra
(*La ben-ta-na noh
ab-reh/s'yer-ra*)

## CAMPING
ACAMPAR

**caravan**
casa rodante/
autocaravana
(*ka*-sa roh-*dan*-teh/
aoo-toh-karra-*va*-na)

**Have you got a list of campsites?**
¿Tiene una lista de sitios para acampar? (*T'yen*-neh oona *lees*-ta deh *seet*-yoss parra a-kam-*parr*)

**Are there any sites available?**
¿Hay sitios disponibles? (*Aee seet*-yoss dees-poh-*nee*-bless)

**How much is it per night/week?**
¿Cuánto cuesta por noche/semana? (*Kwan*-toh *kwess*-ta porr *notch*eh)

**Can we park the caravan here?**
¿Podemos estacionar la casa rodante aquí? (Poh-*deh*-moss es-ta-s'yoh-*narr* la *ka*-sa roh-*dan*-teh a-*kee*)

**Can we camp here overnight?**
¿Podemos acampar aquí por la noche? (Poh-*deh*-moss a-kam-*parr* a-*kee* porr la *notch*eh)

**This site is very muddy**
Este sitio está muy enlodado (*Ess*-te *seet*-yo ess-*ta moo*-ee en-loh-*da*-doh)

**Is there a sheltered site?**
¿Hay un sitio más protegido? (*Aee* oon *seet*-yo *mahss* pro-teh-*khee*-doh)

**Do you have electricity?**
¿Tienen electricidad? (*T'yen*-nen elek-tree-see-*dad*)

**Is there ... in the vicinity?**
¿Hay ... en la vecindad? (*Aee* ... en la beh-seen-*dad*)

◆ **a shop**
◆ una tienda
   (oona t'*yen*-da)

- **a restaurant**
- un restaurante *(oon resta-oo-ran-teh)*

- **an eating place**
- un lugar para comer *(oon loo-garr parra ko-merr)*

- **a garage**
- una gasolinera *(oona gassoh-lee-neh-ra)*

**We'd like to stay for three nights/a week**
Nos gustaría quedarnos por tres noches/una semana *(Nos goos-ta-ree-ya keh-darr-nos porr tress notchess/oona seh-ma-na)*

**Is there drinking water?**
¿Hay agua potable? *(Aee agwa poh-ta-bleh)*

**Can I light a fire here?**
¿Puedo encender fuego aquí? *(Pweh-doh en-sen-derr fweh-goh a-kee)*

**I'd like to buy fire wood**
Me gustaría comprar leña *(Meh goos-ta-ree-a kom-prarr lehn-ya)*

**Is the wood dry?**
¿Está seca la leña? *(Ess-ta seh-ka la lehn-ya)*

**Do you have ... for rent?**
¿Tienen ... para alquilar? *(T'yen-nen ... parra al-kee-larr)*

- **a tent**
- una tienda *(oona t'yen-da)*

- **a gas cylinder**
- una bombona *(oona bom-boh-na)*

- **a groundsheet**
- un aislante para el suelo *(oon aees-lan-teh parra ell sweh-loh)*

**Where is/are the nearest ...?**
¿Dónde está/están ... más cercano? *(Donn-deh ess-ta/ess-tan ... mahss serr-ka-noh)*

- **toilets**
- los servicios *(loss serr-vee-s'yoss)*

- **sink (for dishes)**
- fregadero *(fregga-deh-roh)*

## CUTLERY
### CUBERTERÍA

**knife**
cuchillo *(koo-chee-yoh)*

**fork, cake fork**
tenedor, tenedor de torta
*(ten-eh-dorr, ten-eh-dorr
deh torr-ta)*

**spoon, teaspoon**
cuchara, cucharilla *(koo-
cha-ra, koo-cha-ree-ya)*

**crockery**
vajilla *(ba-khee-ya)*

**plate**
plato *(pla-toh)*

**cup and saucer, mug**
pocillo y platillo, taza
*(poh-see-yo ee
pla-tee-yo, ta-sa)*

## BREAKFAST
### DESAYUNO

**coffee**
café *(ka-feh)*

◆ **black**
◆ solo *(solloh)*

◆ **with milk, cream**
◆ con leche, crema
*(kon letcheh, kreh-ma)*

◆ **without sugar**
◆ sin azúcar *(seen
a-soo-karr)*

**tea**
té *(teh)*

◆ **with milk, lemon**
◆ con leche, limón *(kon
letcheh, lee-mon)*

**bread**
pan *(pan)*

**rolls**
panecillos
*(pa-neh-see-yoss)*

**egg(s)**
huevo(s) *(ooweh-voss)*

◆ **boiled – soft, hard**
◆ pasados por agua –
ligeros, duros
*(pas-sa-doss porr
agwa – lee-khe-ross,
doo-ross)*

◆ **fried**
◆ fritos *(free-toss)*

◆ **scrambled**
◆ revueltos *(rev-wel-toss)*

◆ **poached**
◆ escalfados
(es-kal-_fa_-doss)

◆ **bacon and eggs**
◆ tocino y huevos
(toh-_see_-noh ee
oo_weh_-voss)

**cereal**
cereal (seh-reh-_al_)

**hot milk, cold milk**
leche caliente, leche fría
(_let_cheh kall-_yen_-teh,
_let_cheh _free_-ya)

**fruit**
fruta (_froo_-ta)

**orange juice**
zumo/jugo de naranja
(_soo_-moh/_khoo_-goh deh
na-_ran_-kha)

**jam**
jalea/mermelada
(kha-_leh_-a/mer-meh-_la_-da)

**marmalade**
mermelada
(mer-meh-_la_-da)

**pepper**
pimienta (peem-_yen_-ta)

**salt**
sal (_sal_)

---

**LUNCH/DINNER**
ALMUERZO/
COMIDA/CENA

**Could we have a
table ...?**
¿Tiene una mesa ...?
(T'_yen_-neh oona _meh_-sa)

◆ **by the window**
◆ junto a la ventana
(_khoon_-toh alla
ben-_ta_-na)

◆ **outside**
◆ fuera (_fweh_-ra)

◆ **inside**
◆ dentro (_den_-troh)

**May I have ... ?**
¿Puedo ordenar ... ?
(_Pweh_-doh or-deh-_narr_)

◆ **the wine list**
◆ la carta de vinos (la
_karr_-ta deh _bee_-noss)

◆ **the menu of the day**
◆ el menú del día (ell
meh-_noo_ dell _dee_-ya)

◆ **starters**
◆ entrada/primero
(en-_tra_-da/pree-_meh_-roh

- **main course**
- plato principal/segundo (*pla-toh preen-see-pal/ seh-goon-doh*)

- **dessert**
- postre (*poss-treh*)

- **the menu**
- el menú (*ell meh-noo*)

**I'll take the set menu**
Comeré el menú fijo (*Ko-meh-reh ell meh-noo fee-khoh*)

**What is this?**
¿Qué es ésto? (*Keh ess ess-toh*)

**That is not what I ordered**
Esto no es lo que he ordenado (*Ess-toh noh ess loh keh eh orr-deh-na-doh*)

**It's tough, cold, off**
Está duro, frío, podrido (*Ess-ta doo-roh, free-yoh, pod-ree-doh*)

**What do you recommend?**
¿Qué me recomienda? (*Keh meh rekko-m'yen-da*)

**Can I have the bill please?**
¿Me trae la cuenta, por favor? (*Meh tra-eh la kwen-ta, por fa-vor*)

**We'd like to pay separately**
Queremos pagar en forma separada (*Keh-reh-moss pa-garr en for-ma seppa-ra-da*)

**There is a mistake**
Hay un error (*Aee oon error*)

**Thank you, that's for you**
Gracias, esto es para usted (*Graas-yass, ess-toh ess parra oos-ted*)

**Keep the change**
Quédese con el cambio (*Keh-deh-seh kon ell kam-b'yoh*)

---

**DRINKS**
BEBIDAS

---

**a beer/lager – large, small**
una cerveza – grande, pequeña (*oona serr-veh-sa – grann-deh, peh-kehn-ya*)

**glass (¼ litre) of cider**
una garrafa (un cuarto)
de sidra *(oona gar-raf-fa
[oon kwarr-toh] deh
seed-ra)*

**a dry white wine**
un vino seco
*(oon bee-noh sek-koh)*

**a sweet white wine**
un vino dulce
*(oon bee-noh dool-seh)*

**a light red wine**
un vino tinto ligero
*(oon bee-noh teen-toh
lee-kheh-roh)*

**a full-bodied red
wine**
un vino tinto con cuerpo
*(oon bee-noh teen-toh
kon kwerr-poh)*

**new wine**
vino nuevo *(bee-noh
nweh-voh)*

**house wine**
vino de la casa *(bee-noh
della ka-sa)*

**a glass of wine with
soda water**
un vaso de vino con soda
*(oon ba-soh deh
bee-noh kon soh-da)*

**punch**
ponche *(ponn-cheh)*

**champagne**
espumante
*(es-poo-man-teh)*

**a brandy**
un brandy *(oon brandy)*

**a whisky with ice**
un whisky con hielo *(oon
whisky kon yeh-loh)*

**liqueur**
licor *(lee-korr)*

**a glass**
una copa *(oona kop-pa)*

**a bottle**
una botella
*(oona boh-tey-ya)*

**a mineral water –
still, sparkling**
agua mineral – sin gas,
con gas
*(agwa mee-neh-rall –
seen gass, kon gass)*

**tap water**
agua del grifo
*(agwa dell gree-foh)*

**fruit juice**
zumo de fruta
*(soo-moh deh froo-ta)*

**cola and lemonade**
cola y limonada (*koh*-la ee lee-moh-*na*-da)

**another ... please**
otro ... por favor (*otroh* ... por fa-*vor*)

**too cold**
demasiado frío (*deh*-mass-*ya*-doh *free*-yoh)

**not cold enough**
no está suficientemente frío (*noh* ess-*ta* soo-fee-s'*yen*-teh-*menteh* *free*-yoh)

---

**FOOD**
COMIDA

---

**Soup, Cream Soup**
Sopa, Sopa Crema (*soh*-pa, *soh*-pa *kreh*-ma)

**potato soup, mushroom soup**
sopa de patata/papa, sopa de champiñones (*soh*-pa deh pa-*ta*-ta/ *pappa*, *soh*-pa deh cham-peen-*yoh*-ness)

**cabbage soup**
sopa de repollo (*soh*-pa deh reh-*poy*-yoh

**pea, bean, lentil soup**
sopa de guisantes, judías, lentejas (*soh*-pa deh gee-*san*-tess, khoo-*dee*-yass, len-*teh*-khass

**consommé**
consomé (kon-som-*meh*)

**Fish**
Pescado (pess-*ka*-doh)

**sole**
lenguado (leng-*gwa*-doh)

**plaice**
platija (pla-*tee*-kha)

**cod**
bacalao (ba-ka-*laoo*)

**perch**
perca (*perr*-ca)

**salmon**
salmón (sal-*mon*)

**herring**
arenque (a-*reng*-keh)

**trout**
trucha (*troo*-cha)

**turbot**
rodaballo (roh-da-*baay*-yoh)

**tuna**
atún (a-<u>toon</u>)

**fried, grilled, sautéed**
frito, a la parrilla, salteado
(<u>free</u>-toh, alla pa-<u>reey</u>-ya,
sal-teh-<u>ya</u>-doh)

**POULTRY**
AVES (<u>a</u>-vess)

**chicken**
pollo (<u>poy</u>-yoh)

**crumbed roasted
chicken**
suprema de pollo (soo-
<u>preh</u>-ma deh <u>poy</u>-yoh)

**duck**
pato (<u>pa</u>-toh)

**goose**
ganso (<u>gann</u>-soh)

**roasted**
asado (a-<u>sa</u>-doh)

**MEAT**
CARNE (<u>karr</u>-neh)

**veal**
carne de ternera (<u>karr</u>-
neh deh terr-<u>neh</u>-ra)

**mutton, lamb**
carne de cordero (<u>karr</u>-
neh deh kor-<u>deh</u>-roh)

**beef**
carne de vaca (<u>karr</u>-neh
deh <u>ba</u>-ka)

**pork**
carne de cerdo (<u>karr</u>-neh
deh <u>serr</u>-doh)

**sausage**
salchicha (sal-<u>chee</u>-cha)

**veal sausage**
salchicha de ternera (sal-
<u>chee</u>-cha deh terr-<u>neh</u>-ra)

**venison**
venado (be-<u>na</u>-doh)

**crumbed escalopes**
escalopas apanadas
(es-ka-<u>loh</u>-pass
a-pa-<u>na</u>-dass)

**meat balls/cakes**
bolas de carne
(<u>boh</u>-las deh <u>karr</u>-neh)

**well done, medium,
rare**
bien hecho, medio
hecho, poco hecho
(b'<u>yen</u> <u>etch</u>oh, <u>med</u>-yo
<u>etch</u>oh, <u>poh</u>-koh <u>etch</u>oh)

**boiled, stewed**
hervido, guisado (err-<u>vee</u>-
doh, gee-<u>sa</u>-doh)

**smoked meats**
fiambres ahumados
(f'_yam_-bress aoo-_ma_-doss)

**platter of cold meats**
un plato de fiambres (oon _pla_-toh deh f'_yam_-bress)

**PASTA AND RICE**
PASTA Y ARROZ
(_pas_-ta ee ar-_ross_)

**pasta made with cottage cheese**
pasta hecha con queso untable (_pas_-ta _etcha_ kon _keh_-soh oon-_ta_-bleh)

**pasta with tomato sauce**
pasta con salsa de tomate (_pas_-ta kon _sal_-sa deh toh-_ma_-teh)

**rice**
arroz (ar-_ross_)

**VEGETABLES, SALAD AND FRUIT**
VERDURAS, ENSALADA Y FRUTA (ber-_doo_-rass, en-sa-_la_-da ee _froo_-ta)

**eggplant**
berenjena
(beh-ren-_khe_-na)

**onion**
cebolla (seh-_boy_-ya)

**cabbage**
repollo (reh-_poy_-yoh)

**cauliflower**
coliflor (kollee-_florr_)

**carrots**
zanahorias
(sana-_oh_-r'yas)

**green beans**
judías verdes (khoo-_dee_-yass _berr_-dess)

**leeks**
puerros (_pwer_-ross)

**asparagus**
espárragos
(es-_parra_-goss)

**peppers**
pimiento (peem-_yen_-toh)

**pumpkin**
zapallo, calabaza
(sa-_pay_-yoh, kalla-_ba_-sa)

**potatoes – boiled, fried, mashed**
patatas/papas – hervidas, fritas, puré de papas (pa-_ta_-tass/_pappass_ – err-_vee_-dass, _free_-tass, poo-_reh_ deh _pappass_)

**lettuce**
lechuga (leh-_choo_-ga)

**beetroot**
remolacha (remmo-_la_-cha)

**cucumber**
pepino (peh-_pee_-noh)

**root celery**
apio (_ap_-yoh)

**lemon**
limón (lee-_mon_)

**grapefruit**
pomelo (poh-_meh_-loh)

**apples**
manzanas (man-_sa_-nass)

**pears**
peras (_peh_-rass)

**bananas**
plátanos/bananas
(_pla_-ta-noss, ba-_na_-nass)

**pineapple**
piñas/ananás
(_peen_-yass, a-na-_nass_)

**cherries**
cerezas (seh-_reh_-sass)

**strawberries**
fresas, frutillas
(_freh_-sass, froo-_tee_-yass)

**apricots**
albaricoques/damascos
(al-barree-_koh_-kess,
da-_mass_-koss)

**peaches**
melocotones/duraznos
(melloh-koh-_toh_-ness/
doo-_ras_-noss)

**raspberries**
frambuesas
(fram-_bweh_-sass)

**blackberries**
moras (_moh_-rass)

**plums**
ciruelas (seer-_weh_-lass)

**prunes**
ciruelas pasas
(seer-_weh_-lass _pas_sas)

**grapes**
uvas (_oo_-vass)

**dried fruit**
fruta seca/disecada
(_froo_-ta _seh_-ka/
dee-seh-_ka_-da)

**passion fruit,
grenadilla**
maracuyá (ma-ra-coo-_ya_)

**cranberries**
arándanos (a-_ran_-da-noss)

## DESSERTS AND CAKES
POSTRES Y PASTELES

**fruit salad**
ensalada de frutas (en-sa-_la_-da deh _froo_-tass)

**jelly**
gelatina (khe-la-_tee_-na)

**crème caramel**
flan (_flan_)

**meringue**
merengue (meh-_reng_-geh)

**pastry with apples and raisins**
tarta de manzanas (_tarr_-ta deh man-_sa_-nass)

**light fruitcake**
tarta de frutas (_tarr_-ta deh _froo_-tass)

**plain sponge with crumble topping**
bizcocho (bees-_kotch_oh)

**fruit flan**
flan de frutas (flan deh _froo_-tass)

**marble cake**
torta marmolada (_torr_-ta marr-moh-_la_-da)

**cheesecake**
pastel de queso (pass-_tell_ deh _keh_-soh)

**gateau with cherries and cream**
torta con cerezas y crema (_torr_-ta con seh-_reh_-sass ee _kreh_-ma)

**poppyseed cake**
torta con semillas de amapola (_torr_-ta con seh-_mee_-yass deh amma-_poh_-la)

**honey and almond tart**
tarta de miel y almendras (_tarr_-ta deh _myell_ ee al-_men_-drass)

**sponge cake with chocolate**
bizcocho con chocolate (bees-_kotcho_ con chokkoh-_la_-teh)

**flan with raspberry jam**
flan con jalea de frambuesa (_flan_ con kha-_leh_-ya deh fram-_bweh_-sa)

**gingerbread biscuits**
galletitas de jengibre (ga-yeh-_tee_-tass deh khen-_khee_-breh)

## MONEY
### DINERO

**bureau de change**
cambio/agencia de cambio *(kam-b'yoh/ a-khen-s'ya deh kam-b'yoh)*

**cash dispenser/ATM**
cajero automático *(ka-kheh-roh aoo-toh-ma-tee-koh)*

**Where can I change money?**
¿Dónde puedo cambiar dinero? *(Donn-deh pweh-doh kam-b'yarr dee-neh-roh)*

**Where is an ATM, a bank?**
¿Dónde hay un cajero automático, un banco? *(Donn-deh aee oon ka-kheh-roh aoo-toh-ma-tee-koh, oon bang-koh)*

**When does the bank open/close?**
¿A qué hora abre/cierra el banco? *(A keh oh-ra a-breh/s'yer-ra ell bang-koh)*

**How much commission do you charge?**
¿Cuánta comisión cobran? *(Kwan-ta ko-mee-s'yon kob-ran)*

**I want to ...**
Quiero ... *(Kyeh-roh ...)*

◆ **cash a traveller's cheque**
◆ cambiar cheques de viajero *(kam-b'yarr cheh-kess deh bee-a-kheh-roh)*

◆ **change £50**
◆ cambiar cincuenta libras *(kam-b'yarr seeng-kwen-ta lee-brass)*

◆ **make a transfer**
◆ hacer una transferencia *(a-serr oona trans-feh-ren-s'ya)*

### POST OFFICE
#### OFICINA DE CORREOS

**How much is ...?**
¿Cuánto cuesta ...? *(Kwan-toh kwess-ta)*

◆ **a letter**
◆ una carta *(oona karr-ta)*

◆ **a postcard to ...**
◆ una postal a ...
*(oona poss-tal a ...)*

◆ **a small parcel**
◆ un paquete pequeño
*(oon pa-keh-teh
peh-kehn-yoh)*

**Where can I buy
stamps?**
¿Dónde puedo comprar
sellos? *(Donn-deh pweh-
doh kom-prarr sey-yoss)*

---

### SHOPPING
COMPRAS

---

**What does it cost?**
¿Cuánto cuesta? *(Kwan-
toh kwess-ta)*

**How much is it (total)?**
¿Cuánto es todo?
*(Kwan-toh ess toddoh)*

**I need a receipt**
Necesito un recibo
*(ne-seh-see-toh oon
reh-see-boh)*

**Do you accept credit
cards?**
¿Se aceptan tarjetas de
crédito? *(Seh a-sep-tan
tarr-kheh-tass deh
kreh-dee-toh)*

**Do you take trav-
eller's cheques?**
¿Se aceptan cheques de
viajero? *(Seh a-sep-tan
cheh-kess deh
bee-a-kheh-roh)*

**Where do I pay?**
¿Dónde pago?
*(Donn-deh pa-goh)*

**Does that include
VAT?**
¿El IVA está incluido?
*(Ell ee oo-veh a ess-ta
een-kloo-ee-doh)*

**Do you need a
deposit?**
¿Necesita un depósito?
*(ne-seh-see-ta oon
deh-poh-see-toh)*

**Can you wrap it up
for me?**
¿Puedes envolverlo?
*(Pweh-dess
em-bol-verr-loh)*

**This isn't what I want**
Esto no es lo que yo
quiero *(Ess-toh noh ess
loh keh yoh k'yeh-roh)*

**This isn't correct (bill)**
Esto no es correcto (la
cuenta)*(Ess-toh noh ess
koh-rek-toh)*

**I want my money back**
Quiero de vuelta mi dinero (K'_yeh_-roh deh _bwell_-ta mee dee-_neh_-roh)

**This is ...**
Esto está ... (_Ess_-toh ess-_ta_ ...)

◆ **broken**
◆ roto (_roh_-toh)

◆ **damaged**
◆ dañado (dan-_ya_-doh

**Can you repair it?**
¿Puede repararlo? (_Pweh_-deh reppa-_rarr_-loh)

**BUYING FOOD**
COMPRA DE COMIDA

**Where can I buy ...?**
¿Dónde puedo comprar ...? (_Donn_-deh _pweh_-doh kom-_prarr_)

◆ **bread**
◆ pan (_pan_)

◆ **cake**
◆ pastel/torta (pass-_tell_/ _torr_-ta)

◆ **cheese**
◆ queso (_keh_-soh)

◆ **butter**
◆ mantequilla (man-teh-_kee_-ya)

◆ **milk**
◆ leche (_letcheh_)

◆ **water**
◆ agua (_agwa_)

◆ **wine**
◆ vino (_bee_-noh)

◆ **sparkling wine**
◆ vino espumante (_bee_-noh es-poo-_man_-teh)

◆ **beer**
◆ cerveza (serr-_veh_-sa)

◆ **fruit juice**
◆ jugo/zumo de fruta (_khoo_-goh/_soo_-moh deh _froo_-ta)

◆ **meat**
◆ carne (_karr_-neh)

◆ **ham**
◆ jamón (kha-_monn_)

◆ **polony/cold meats**
◆ fiambres (_fyam_-bress)

◆ **vegetables**
◆ verduras (ber-_doo_-rass)

- **fruit**
- fruta (*froo-ta*)

- **eggs**
- huevos (*ooweh-voss*)

**I'll take ...**
Llevo ... (*Yeh-voh ...*)

- **one kilo**
- un kilo (*oon kee-loh*)

- **three slices**
- tres rebanadas (*tress rebba-na-dass*)

- **a portion of**
- una porción de (*oona por-s'yon deh*)

- **a packet of**
- un paquete de (*oon pa-keh-teh deh*)

- **a dozen**
- una docena (*oona doh-seh-na*)

### BUYING CLOTHES
COMPRA DE ROPA

**Can I try this on?**
¿Puedo probarlo? (*Pweh-doh proh-barr-loh*)

**It is ...**
Es ... (*Ess ...*)

- **too big**
- demasiado grande (*deh-mass-ya-doh grann-deh*)

- **too small**
- demasiado pequeño (*deh-mass-ya-doh peh-kehn-yoh*)

- **too tight**
- demasiado ajustado (*deh-mass-ya-doh a-khoos-ta-doh*)

- **too wide**
- demasiado ancho (*deh-mass-ya-doh anchoh*)

- **too expensive**
- demasiado caro (*deh-mass-ya-doh ka-roh*)

**I'll take ...**
Llevo ... (*Yeh-voh ...*)

- **this one**
- éste/ésta (*ess-teh/ess-ta*)

- **size 40**
- talla 40 (*tay-ya kwa-ren-ta*)

- **two**
- dos (*doss*)

## CLOTHING SIZES – TALLAS DE ROPA

**Women's Wear**

| UK | Cont. Europe | USA |
|----|--------------|-----|
| 10 | 38 | 8 |
| 12 | 40 | 10 |
| 14 | 42 | 12 |
| 16 | 44 | 14 |
| 18 | 46 | 16 |

**Menswear**

| UK | Cont. Europe | USA |
|----|--------------|-----|
| 36 | 46 | 36 |
| 38 | 48 | 38 |
| 40 | 50 | 40 |
| 42 | 52 | 42 |
| 44 | 54 | 44 |
| 46 | 56 | 46 |

**Men's Shirts**

| UK | Cont. Europe | USA |
|----|--------------|-----|
| 14 | 36 | 14 |
| 14.5 | 37 | 14.5 |
| 15 | 38 | 15 |
| 15.5 | 39 | 15.5 |
| 16 | 41 | 16 |
| 17 | 43 | 17 |

**Shoes**

| UK | Cont. Europe | USA |
|----|--------------|-----|
| 5 | 39 | 6 |
| 6 | 40 | 7 |
| 7 | 41 | 8 |
| 8 | 42 | 9 |
| 9 | 43 | 10 |
| 10 | 44 | 11 |
| 11 | 45 | 12 |

## SIGHTSEEING
TURISMO

**tourist office**
oficina de turismo *(offee-see-na deh too-rees-moh)*

**Do you have brochures/leaflets?**
¿Tiene folletos? *(T'yen-neh foy-yeh-toss)*

**I/We want to visit ...**
Queremos visitar ...
*(Kehr-reh-moss bee-see-tarr ...)*

**When is it open/closed?**
¿A qué hora abre/cierra?
*(A keh oh-ra ab-reh/ s'yer-ra)*

**What does it cost?**
¿Cuánto cuesta?
*(Kwan-toh kwess-ta)*

**Are there any reductions for ...?**
¿Hay descuento para ...?
*(Aee des-kwen-toh parra)*

- **children**
- niños *(neen-yoss)*

- **senior citizens**
- jubilados
  *(khoo-bee-la-doss)*

- **students**
- estudiantes
  *(es-toodee-yan-tess)*

**Are there any tours?**
¿Hay visitas guiadas?
*(Aee bee-see-tass gee-ya-dass)*

**When does the bus depart/return?**
¿Cuándo sale/regresa el autobús? *(Kwan-doh sa-leh/reh-gres-sa ell aoo-toh-booss)*

**From where does the bus leave?**
¿De dónde sale el autobús? *(Deh donn-deh sa-leh ell aoo-toh-booss)*

**Where is the museum?**
¿Dónde está el museo?
*(Donn-deh ess-ta ell moo-seh-yoh)*

**How much is the entrance fee?**
¿Cuánto cuesta la entrada? *(Kwan-toh kwess-ta la en-tra-da)*

## ENTERTAINMENT
DIVERSIÓN

**Is there a list of cultural events?**
¿Hay una lista/guía de eventos culturales?
(*Aee oona lees-ta/gee-ya deh eh-ven-toss kool-too-ra-less*)

**Are there any festivals?**
¿Hay algún festival?
(*Aee al-goon fes-tee-val*)

**I'd like to go to ...**
Quiero ir ... (*K'yeh-roh eer ...*)

♦ **the theatre**
♦ al teatro (*al teh-a-tro*)

♦ **the opera**
♦ a la ópera
(*alla oh-peh-ra*)

♦ **the ballet**
♦ al ballet (*al ba-yeh*)

♦ **the cinema/movies**
♦ al cine (*al see-neh*)

♦ **a concert**
♦ a un concierto
(*a oon kon-s'yer-toh*)

**Do I have to book?**
¿Debo reservar?
(*Debboh reh-ser-varr*)

**How much are the tickets?**
¿Cuánto cuestan los billetes? (*Kwan-toh kwess-tan loss bee-yet-tess*)

**Two tickets for ...**
Dos billetes para ... (*Doss bee-yet-tess parra*)

♦ **tonight**
♦ esta noche (*ess-ta notcheh*)

♦ **tomorrow night**
♦ mañana por la noche
(*man-ya-na porr la notcheh*)

♦ **the early show**
♦ la matiné (*la ma-tee-neh*)

♦ **the late show**
♦ el espectáculo más tarde (*ell es-pek-ta-coo-loh mahss tarr-deh*)

**When does the performance start/end?**
¿A qué hora comienza/termina la función? (*A keh oh-ra koh-m'yen-sa/terr-mee-na la foon-s'yon*)

**Where is ...?**
¿Dónde hay ...?
(_Donn_-deh _aee_ ...)

- **a good bar**
- un buen bar (oon _bwen_ barr)

- **good live music**
- buena música en vivo (_bweh_-na _moo_-see-ka en _bee_-voh)

**Is it ...?**
Es/Está ...? (_Ess_/Ess-_ta_ ...)

- **expensive**
- caro (_ka_-roh)

- **noisy, crowded**
- ruidoso, muy lleno (rooee-_doh_-soh, mooee _yen_-noh)

**How do I get there?**
¿Cómo llego allí? (_kom_-moh _yeh_-goh a-_yee_)

---

**SPORT**
DEPORTES

---

**Where can we ...?**
¿Dónde podemos ...?
(_Donn_-deh poh-_deh_-moss)

- **go skiing**
- esquiar (es-kee-_yarr_)

- **play tennis/golf**
- jugar al tenis/golf (khoo-_garr_ al _ten_-nees/golf)

- **go swimming**
- nadar (na-_darr_)

- **go fishing**
- pescar (pess-_karr_)

- **go riding**
- cabalgar (ka-bal-_garr_)

- **go cycling**
- andar/montar en bicicleta (an-_darr_/mon-_tarr_ en bee-see-_kleh_-ta)

- **hire bicycles**
- alquilar bicicletas (al-kee-_larr_ bee-see-_kleh_-tass)

- **hire tackle**
- alquilar equipos de pesca (al-kee-_larr_ eh-_kee_-poss deh _pess_-ka)

- **hire golf clubs**
- alquilar palos de golf (al-kee-_larr_ pa-loss deh _golf_)

- **hire skis**
- alquilar esquís (al-kee-_larr_ es-_keess_)

- **hire a boat**
- alquilar un barco/un bote/una lancha (al-kee-_larr_ oon _barr_-koh/ oon _boh_-teh/ oona _lan_-cha)

- **hire skates**
- alquilar patines (al-kee-_larr_ pa-_tee_-ness)

- **hire an umbrella**
- alquilar un parasol/ sombrilla (al-kee-_larr_ oon parra-_sol_/ som-_bree_-ya)

- **hire a deck chair**
- alquilar una silla para el sol (al-kee-_larr_ oona _see_-ya parra ell sol)

**How much is it ...?**
¿Cuánto cuesta ...? (_Kwan_-toh _kwess_-ta ...)

- **per hour**
- por hora (porr _oh_-ra)

- **per day**
- por día (porr _dee_-ya)

- **per session/game**
- por sesión/juego (porr sess-_yon_/kh_weh_-goh)

**Is it ...?**
Es ...? (_Ess_ ...)

- **deep**
- profundo (proh-_foon_-doh)

- **clean**
- limpio (_leem_-pyoh)

- **cold**
- frío (_free_-yoh)

**How do we get there?**
¿Cómo llegamos allí? (_Koh_-moh yeh-_ga_-moss a-_yee_)

**No swimming/diving**
Prohibido nadar/zambullirse (Pro-ee-_bee_-doh na-_darr_/sam-boo-_yeer_-seh)

**Are there currents?**
¿Hay corrientes? (_Aee_ korr-_yen_-tess)

**Do I need a fishing permit?**
¿Necesito un permiso de pesca? (Ne-seh-_see_-toh oon per-_mee_-soh deh _pess_-ka)

**Where can I get one?**
¿Dónde puedo obtenerlo? (_Donn_-deh _pweh_-doh ob-teh-_nerr_-lo)

# ACTIVIDADES

## Is there a guide for walks?
¿Hay un guía para las caminatas? (_Aee_ oon _gee_-ya parra lass kamee-_na_-tass)

## Do I need walking boots?
¿Necesito botas para senderismo? (neh-seh-_see_-toh _boh_-tass parra sen-deh-_rees_-moh)

## How much is a ski pass?
¿Cuánto cuesta un pase de esquí? (_Kwan_-toh _kwess_-ta oon _pa_-seh deh es-_kee_)

## Is it safe to ski today?
¿Es seguro esquiar hoy? (Ess seh-_goo_-roh es-kee-_yarr_ oy)

## Run closed
Pista cerrada (_Pees_-ta ser-_ra_-da)

## avalanches
avalanchas (ava-_lan_-chass)

## I'm a beginner
Soy principiante (_Soy_ preen-see-pee-_an_-teh)

## Danger
Peligro (peh-_lee_-groh)

## Which is an easy run?
¿Cuál es una pista fácil? (_Kwal_ ess oona _pees_-ta _fa_-seel)

## My skis are too long/short
Mis esquís son demasiado largos/cortos (Mees es-_keess_ sonn de-mass-_ya_-doh _larr_-goss/_korr_-toss)

## We want to go ...
Queremos ir ... (Keh-_reh_-moss eer ...)

◆ **hiking**
◆ de senderismo/de caminata (deh sen-deh-_rees_-moh/ deh kamee-_na_-ta)

◆ **sailing**
◆ a navegar (a na-veh-_garr_)

◆ **ice-skating**
◆ a patinar sobre hielo (a pa-tee-_narr_ sob-breh _yeh_-loh)

◆ **water-skiing**
◆ a hacer esquí acuático (a a-_serr_ es-_kee_ akoo-_a_-tee-koh)

## PHARMACY/ CHEMIST
FARMACIA

**health shop**
tienda de medicinas
naturales *(t'yen-da deh
meddee-see-nass
na-too-ra-less)*

**Have you got
something for ...?**
¿Tiene algo para ...?
*(T'yn-neh al-goh parra ...)*

◆ **diarrhoea**
◆ diarrea *(dee-ya-reh-ya)*

◆ **cold, flu**
◆ resfriado, gripe *(ress-
free-a-doh, gree-peh)*

◆ **headache**
◆ dolor de cabeza
*(doh-lorr de ka-beh-sa)*

◆ **a sore throat**
◆ dolor de garganta
*(doh-lorr de
garr-gan-ta)*

◆ **stomachache**
◆ dolor de estómago
*(doh-lorr de
es-toh-ma-goh)*

◆ **car sickness**
◆ mareo de viaje en
coche *(ma-reh-yoh
deh bee-a-kheh en
kotcheh)*

**I need ...**
Necesito ...
*(Ne-seh-see-toh ...)*

◆ **indigestion tablets**
◆ tabletas para
indigestión
*(tab-leh-tass parra
een-dee-khess-t'yon)*

◆ **laxative**
◆ laxativo *(lax-a-tee-voh)*

◆ **sleeping tablets**
◆ tabletas para dormir
*(tab-leh-tass parra
dorr-meer)*

◆ **a painkiller**
◆ un analgésico *(oon
annal-kheh-see-koh)*

**Is it safe for
children?**
¿Es seguro para niños?
*(Ess seh-goo-roh parra
neen-yoss)*

**I'm a diabetic**
Soy diabético *(Soy
dee-ya-bet-tee-koh)*

**I have high blood pressure**
Sufro de presión alta
(*Soo*-froh deh
pres-see-*on* alta)

**I'm allergic to ...**
Soy alérgico a ... (Soy
a-*lerr*-khee-koh a ...)

**I am ill**
Estoy enfermo
(*Estoy* en-*ferr*-moh)

**I need a doctor**
Necesito un médico
(Ne-seh-*see*-toh oon
*med*-dee-koh)

**He/she has a high temperature**
Tiene fiebre
(T'*yen*-neh fee-*eb*-reh)

**It hurts**
Duele (*Dweh*-leh)

**I am going to be sick!**
¡Voy a vomitar!
(Boy a bo-mee-*tarr*)

**dentist**
dentista (den-*tees*-ta)

**I have toothache**
Me duelen los dientes
(Meh *dweh*-len loss
dee-*en*-tess)

**optometrist**
optometrista
(op-toh-meh-*trees*-ta)

**Will I have to go to hospital?**
¿Debo ir al
hospital?(*Debboh* eer
al oss-pee-*tal*)

**Where is the hospital?**
¿Dónde está el hospital?
(*Donn*-deh ess-*ta*
ell oss-pee-*tal*)

**Which ward?**
¿Cuál sala? (*Kwal sa*-la)

**When are visiting hours?**
¿Cuál es el horario de
visita? (*Kwal* ess ell oh-
*raar*-yoh deh *bee*-see-ta)

**Where is casualty?**
¿Dónde están las urgen-
cias? (*Donn*-deh ess-*tan*
lass oor-khens-yass)

## POLICE
POLICÍA

**Call the police**
Llame a la policía *(Ya-meh alla pollee-see-ya)*

**I have been robbed**
Me han robado
*(Meh an ro-ba-doh)*

**My car has been stolen**
Han robado mi coche *(An ro-ba-doh mee kotcheh)*

**My car has been broken into**
Han robado de mi coche *(An ro-ba-doh deh mee kotcheh)*

**I want to report a theft**
Quiero denunciar un robo *(K'yeh-roh deh-noon-see-yarr oon roh-boh)*

**I have been attacked**
Me han atacado
*(Meh an atta-ka-doh)*

**I have been raped**
Me han violado
*(Meh an bee-oh-la-doh)*

**Where is the police station?**
¿Dónde está la oficina de policía/comisaría? *(Donn-deh ess-ta la offee-see-na deh pollee-see-ya)*

## EMERGENCIES
EMERGENCIAS

**Call an ambulance**
Llame una ambulancia *(Ya-meh oona amboo-lan-s'ya)*

**There's been an accident**
Hubo un accidente *(Oo-boh oon ak-see-den-teh)*

**Someone is injured**
Alguien está herido *(Al-gee-yen ess-ta eh-ree-doh)*

**Hurry up!**
¡Date prisa!
*(Da-teh pree-sa)*

**Could you please help me?**
¿Puede ayudarme por favor? *(Pweh-deh a-yoo-darr-meh por fa-vor)*

**Help!**
¡Ayúdeme!
(a-_yoo_-deh-meh)

**This is an emergency!**
¡Hay una emergencia!
(_Aee_ oona
em-merr-_khen_-s'ya)

**My son/daughter is missing**
Mi hijo/hija está desaparecido/a
(Mee _ee_-khoh/_ee_-kha
ess-_ta_ dessa-parreh-_see_-doh/da)

**I need a report for my insurance**
Necesito un informe para mi seguro (Ne-seh-_see_-toh oon een-_forr_-meh parra mee seh-_goo_-roh)

**I want to phone my embassy**
Quiero llamar a mi embajada (K'_yeh_-roh _ya_-_marr_ mee em-ba-_kha_-da)

**I am lost**
Estoy perdido
(Es_toy_ per-_dee_-doh)

**He/she is ill**
Está enfermo/a
(Ess-_ta_ en-_ferr_-moh/ma)

---

**FIRE DEPARTMENT**
BOMBEROS

**Fire!**
¡Fuego! (_Fweh_-goh)

**Look out!**
¡Cuídese! (_Kee_-deh-seh)

**Call the fire department**
Llame a los bomberos
(_Ya_-meh a loss bom-_beh_-ross)

**It's an electrical fire**
Es un incendio eléctrico
(Ess oon een-_senn_-d'yoh _elek_-tree-koh)

**The address is ...**
La dirección es ... (La dee-rek-s'_yon_ ess ...)

**I need ...**
Necesito ...
(Ne-seh-_see_-toh ...)

♦ **a fire extinguisher**
♦ un extintor
  (oon ex-_teen_-torr)

♦ **medical assistance**
♦ ayuda médica
  (a-_yoo_-da _meh_-dee-ka)

## THE HUMAN BODY
### EL CUERPO HUMANO

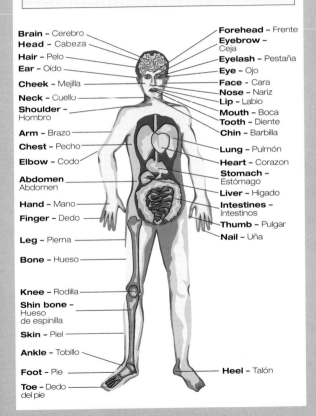

**Brain** – Cerebro
**Head** – Cabeza
**Hair** – Pelo
**Ear** – Oído
**Cheek** – Mejilla
**Neck** – Cuello
**Shoulder** – Hombro
**Arm** – Brazo
**Chest** – Pecho
**Elbow** – Codo
**Abdomen** – Abdomen
**Hand** – Mano
**Finger** – Dedo
**Leg** – Pierna
**Bone** – Hueso
**Knee** – Rodilla
**Shin bone** – Hueso de espinilla
**Skin** – Piel
**Ankle** – Tobillo
**Foot** – Pie
**Toe** – Dedo del pie

**Forehead** – Frente
**Eyebrow** – Ceja
**Eyelash** – Pestaña
**Eye** – Ojo
**Face** - Cara
**Nose** – Nariz
**Lip** – Labio
**Mouth** – Boca
**Tooth** – Diente
**Chin** – Barbilla
**Lung** – Pulmón
**Heart** – Corazon
**Stomach** – Estómago
**Liver** – Hígado
**Intestines** – Intestinos
**Thumb** – Pulgar
**Nail** – Uña
**Heel** – Talón

75

## FORMS OF ADDRESS
TRATOS

There are two ways of translating the English word 'you'. The formal way is *Usted* (which is abbreviated *Ud.*). This form of address is a sign of courtesy and respect, and would normally be used when addressing elderly people, teachers, bosses, shopkeepers and people you don't know very well, especially if they are older than you.

The less formal translation of 'you' is *tú*, which is the form generally used when addressing family, friends and people you know well. Nowadays *tú* is used much more often than before.

## GREETING PEOPLE
SALUDOS

When it comes to greeting each other, the Hispanic people are rather formal, and the usual form of greeting is to shake hands. This applies to both young and old people.

Hugging is also a very Hispanic custom, and men who know each other well will usually hug each other.

Kissing varies from country to country. In Spain a greeting will usually consist of two kisses, one on each cheek, whereas in most Latin American countries there will only be one kiss on the cheek.

Eye contact is important, and Latinos expect you to make eye contact whenever you speak to them. In many societies it is in fact considered rude not to establish and maintain eye contact.

## MANNERS
ETIQUETA

The well-known fiery Latin temperament means that Spanish people are usually quite outspoken and direct. This same tempera-ment also leads to rather high levels of noise. The people speak loudly, and the drivers generally hoot a lot, so don't expect an especially quiet time when visiting a Spanish-speaking country!

On the other hand, there is the very Spanish custom of the *siesta*, and in most Spanish-speaking countries everything comes to a standstill during the hottest part of the day, when people have a rest.

Spanish-speaking people can be very helpful towards strangers. The more you try to talk to them, no matter how excruciating your Spanish pronunciation is, the more they will want to help you. They may even offer to acompany you to whichever place it is you are trying to find. So it would be well worth your while to learn the basics of the language before you embark on a visit to a Spanish-speaking country, whether you are going on holiday or on a business trip. If you make the effort it will be appreciated.

## COMMUNICATION
COMUNICACIÓN
There are many Spanish words that cannot be simply and literally translated into English, for example words such as *relación* (relationship), *comida* (food) or *paseo* (a walk), which have many more connotations attached to them than their literal meanings tell us.

The Spanish phrase *dar un paseo*, for instance, literally means 'to go for a walk', but it carries with it a wealth of social images such as people out for a leisurely walk with their family and friends, sitting and relaxing at a sidewalk café, seeing people and in turn being seen by others. In Spanish-speaking countries to go for a walk means something entirely different to what it means to English-speaking people.

## FOOD AND MEALS
COMIDAS

Just as the geography of the Hispanic world is very extensive, so too is its cuisine. If you talk about Spanish food in the United States of America, you are probably referring to Mexican food. But the food in Mexico is very different from the food in Spain. Many Mexican dishes are based on the tortilla. The Mexican tortilla is a pancake made of maize, whereas the Spanish tortilla is an omelette made of potatoes. In the same way there are many differences between Mexican food and Chilean food, as there are between Chilean food and Argentinian food.

In Spain you will be able to sample a wide variety of delicious *tapas*, or snacks. These can range from a simple dish of olives to more elegant offerings such as bits of spicy sausage, meatballs in sauce, various cheeses or beautifully prepared fish snacks. The name *tapas* literally means 'lids', as these snacks originated in the 19th century when bartenders used to place a small dish of nuts on top of a beer glass, probably to keep the flies out!

Spain is also famous for its *paella*, a wonderful dish based on rice with the addition of meat, seafood and vegetables. The name comes from the Spanish *para ella*, meaning 'for her'. The dish originated from the old custom of husbands taking over the cooking duties from their wives on a Sunday in order to give the lady of the house a well-earned break. The elegant *paella* you will encounter in restaurants nowadays probably bears little resemblance to the concoction from whence it came, because the original *paella* was made with whatever leftovers the man of the house could lay his hands on, whereas today it is made with fresh ingredients.

Meal times vary enormously from country to country and also from season to season. Dinner is usually quite late – in most cases well after 20:00 and often as late as 22:00 – especially in summer.

**New Year's Day**
*Día de año nuevo*
(1 January)
Exuberant parties and dances are held on 31 December – *la noche de año viejo* – so most people spend New Year's Day recovering.

**Epiphany**
*Epifanía del Señor*
(6 January)
A religious holiday commemorating the manifestation of Christ to the Three Kings.

**Easter**
*Semana Santa*
(March/April)
The Easter weekend includes Good Friday – *Viernes Santo* – which is preceded by *Jueves Santo* ('Good Thursday'), as well as Easter Sunday (*Domingo de Pascua*) and Easter Monday (*Lunes Santo*). Special Easter church services are held all over Spain.

**May Day, Labour Day**
*Fiesta del Trabajo*
(1 May)
An official holiday for the workers.

**All Saints' Day**
*Todos los Santos*
(1 November)
A religious holiday celebrated by Christians to honour all the saints.

**Spanish Constitution Day** – *Día de la Constitución Española* (6 December)
Celebrates the Spanish Constitution of 1978, which was the culmination of the Spanish transition to democracy.

**Immaculate Conception**
*Concepto Inmaculado* (8 December)
A religious holiday commemorating the conception of Christ.

**Christmas**
*Navidad* (25 December)
From the first Sunday of Advent private and public festivities mark this special season, leading up to the highlight of Christmas Eve (*Nochebuena*).

**REGIONAL HOLIDAYS**
FIESTAS REGIONALES

*Día de la Convivencia* (31 January)
Ceuta.

*Día de Andalucía* (28 February)
Andalucía.

*Día de las Islas Baleares* (1 March)
Balearic Islands.

*Fiesta Comunidad de Madrid* (2 May)
Madrid.

**Día Letras Gallegas**
(17 May)
Galicia.

**Día Islas Canarias**
(30 May)
Canary Islands.

**Día Regional de La Mancha**
(31 May)
La Mancha.

**Día Regional de Murcia**
(9 June)
Murcia.

**Día Regional La Rioja**
(9 June)
La Rioja.

**Santiago Apostol**
(25 July)
A regional holiday celebrated in Castilla León, Galicia, Navarra and Basque Country.

**Día Institucional de Cantabria**
(28 July)
Cantabria.

**Día de Asturias**
(8 September)
Asturias.

**Día de Extremadura**
(11 September)
Extremadura.

**Nuestra Señora Bien Aparecida**
(15 September)
Cantabria.

**Día Comunidad Valenciana**
(9 October)
Valencia.

## NATIONAL DAYS
FIESTAS NACIONALES

*Fiesta Nacional Española* (12 October)
Spanish National Day.

Other national days:
27 February **Dominican Republic**
14 May **Paraguay**
25 May **Argentina**
5 July **Venezuela**
20 July **Colombia**
28 July **Peru**
6 August **Bolivia**
10 August **Ecuador**
25 August **Uruguay**
15 September **Costa Rica, El Salvador, Guatemala, Honduras, Nicaragua**
16 September **Mexico**
18 September **Chile**
12 October **Equatorial Guinea**

## SPECIAL FESTIVALS
FESTIVALES ESPECIALES

*Las Fallas*
(begins on the first Sunday of March)
Valencia, Spain.
This lively festival commemorates St Joseph's Day (the patron saint of carpenters). Enormous elaborate figures are built from wood and papier-mâché and then burned on the last day of the fiesta. Teams of carpenters, artists and craftsmen spend a year building these statues, and the burning is accompanied by much cheering from the crowd.

### Abril Feria
(last week in April)
Seville, Spain.
Much dancing, eating and drinking takes place during Seville's annual April Fair. The local people dress up in traditional costumes and the festivities last the whole week.

### Fiesta de San Fermin
(second week in July)
Pamplona, Spain.
The famous 'Running of the Bulls' through the streets of Pamplona is probably the best-known and most popular celebration in Spain. The festival also includes fireworks, wine tasting and, of course, bullfights.

### La Tomatina
(last Wednesday in August)
Buñol, Spain.
Every year at the height of summer thousands of people descend on the town of Buñol (located in Spain's Valencia region) to throw tons of tomatoes at each other as part of this rather bizarre festival.

### Día de la Raza
(nearest Monday to 12 October)
Columbus Day (Race Day) is celebrated in Argentina, Costa Rica, Ecuador, Honduras, Venezuela, Uruguay, Mexico and Chile, to mark Columbus's discovery of America.

ENGLISH → SPANISH

## A

**abbey** abadía f
**abortion** aborto m
**about (approximately)** aproximadamente
**above** sobre
**abroad** en el extranjero
**abscess** absceso m
**absolutely** por supuesto, claro
**accelerator** acelerador m
**accent** acento m
**accept** aceptar
**accident** accidente m
**accommodation** alojamiento m
**account** cuenta f
**accurate** exacto
**ache** dolor m
**adapter** adaptador m
**adhesive tape** cinta adhesiva f
**admission fee** entrada f
**adult (adj, n)** adulto/a m/f
**advance, in advance** por adelantado
**advertisement** aviso m
**advice** consejo m
**advise** aconsejar
**aeroplane** avión m
**afraid, be afraid of** tener miedo
**after** después
**afternoon** tarde

**afterwards** después, luego
**again** otra vez
**against** contra
**age** edad f
**agree** estar de acuerdo
**agreement** acuerdo m
**air** aire m
**air conditioning** aire acondicionado
**air ticket** billete aéreo
**airmail** correo aéreo
**airport** aeropuerto m
**aisle** pasillo m
**aisle seat** asiento en el pasillo
**all right** vale, está bien
**allow** permitir, dejar
**almond** almendra f
**almost** casi
**alone** solo
**already** ya
**also** también
**although** a pesar de
**altogether** todo junto
**always** siempre
**a.m. (before noon)** por la mañana
**am, I am** yo soy/estoy
**amazing** fabuloso, maravilloso
**amber** ámbar m
**ambulance** ambulancia f
**among** dentro
**amount** monto m, cantidad f
**anaesthetic** anestético m

**ancient** viejo/a
**and** y
**angry** enfadado, enojado
**animal** animal **m**
**ankle** tobillo **m**
**anniversary**
  aniversario **m**
**annoy** molestar
**annual** anual
**another** otro/a
**answer (n)** respuesta **f**
**answer (vb)** responder
**ant** hormiga
**antacid** antiácido
**anybody** cualquiera
**anything** cualquier cosa
**apartment** piso **m**,
  apartemento **m**
**apology** disculpa **f**
**appendicitis** apendicitis **f**
**appointment** cita **f**
**approximately**
  aproximadamente
**apron** delantal **m**
**are** son, están
**area** barrio **m**, área **f**
**armchair** sillón **m**
**arrange** arreglar
**arrest** arrestar
**arrival** llegada **f**
**arrive** llegar
**art** arte **m**
**artist** artista **m/f**
**ask** preguntar
**astonishing** fascinante
**at** en
**attack (n)** ataque **m**
**attack (vb)** atacar

**attic** ático **m**
**audience** audiencia **f**
**aunt** tía **f**
**auto-teller** cajero
  automático
**autumn** otoño **m**
**available** disponible
**avalanche** avalancha **f**
**avenue** avenida **f**
**average** promedio
**avoid** evitar
**awake** despertar
**away** fuera
**awful** feo/a, malo/a,
  terrible

**B**
**baby food** comida
  para bebé
**back** espalda **f**
**backache** dolor de
  espalda
**backpack** mochila **f**
**bacon** tocino **m**
**bad** malo/a
**bag** bolsa **f**
**baggage** equipaje **m**
**baggage reclaim**
  recolección de equipajes
**bait** cebo **m**, carnada **f**
**bakery** panadería **f**
**balcony** balcón **m**
**ballpoint pen**
  bolígrafo **m**, lapicera
**Baltic Sea** Mar Báltico
**bandage** venda **f**,
  vendaje **m**

**ENGLISH → SPANISH**

**bar of chocolate**
barra de chocolate
**barber's shop** barbería f
**bark (vb)** ladrar
**barn** granero m
**barrel** barril m
**basement** sótano m
**basket** cesta, canasta f
**bath** bañera f
**bathroom** baño m,
servicios mpl
**bay** bahía f
**bay leaf** hoja de laurel
**be** ser, estar
**beach** playa f
**bean** haba f, judía f,
frijol m
**beard** barba f
**beautiful** bonito/a,
precioso/a, lindo/a
**beauty salon**
salón de belleza
**because** porque
**because of** por
**bed** cama f
**bed & breakfast**
pensión f
**bed linen** ropa de cama
**bedspread** cobertor
**bee** abeja f
**beef** carne de vaca f
**beer** cerveza f
**before** antes
**beginner** principiante m/f
**behind** detrás
**Belgian (adj, n)**
belga m/f
**Belgium** Bélgica

**believe** creer
**bell** campana f
**below** bajo
**belt** cinturón m
**bend** doblar
**beside** junto a
**bet** apostar
**better** mejor
**beyond** más allá
**bicycle** bicicleta f
**big** gran, grande
**bill** cuenta f
**bin** cubo de la basura
**binoculars** binoculares,
prismáticos mpl
**bird** pájaro m, ave f
**birth** nacimiento m
**birth certificate**
certificado de nacimiento
**birthday** cumpleaños m
**birthday card** tarjeta
de cumpleaños
**birthday present**
regalo de cumpleaños
**biscuit** galleta f
**bit** un poco
**bite (vb)** morder
**black** negro/a
**blackcurrant**
grosella negra
**blanket** manta f
**bleach (vb)** blanquear
**bleed** sangrar
**blind (n)** persiana
**blind (adj)** ciego/a
**blister** ampolla f
**block of flats** edificio
de apartamentos

ENGLISH → SPANISH

**blocked** cerrado/a, bloqueado
**blood** sangre f
**blood pressure** presión arterial
**blouse** blusa f
**blow-dry** secar
**blue** azul
**blunt** contundente
**blusher** colorete m
**boar** jabalí m
**boarding card** tarjeta de embarque
**boarding house** pensión f
**boat** barco m, bote m
**boat trip** viaje en barco
**body** cuerpo m
**boil (n)** furúnculo m
**boil (vb)** hervir
**bone** hueso m
**bonnet (car)** capó/capota m/f
**book** libro m
**bookshop** librería f
**boots** botas fpl
**border** borde m
**boring** aburrido, pesado/a
**born** nacer
**borrow** tomar prestado
**both** los dos, ambos
**bottle** botella f
**bottle opener** abridor de botellas
**bottom (at the)** al fondo
**bow tie** humita, pajarita f

**bowl** cuenco m
**box** caja f
**boy** niño m
**boyfriend** novio m
**bra** sostén m
**bracelet** pulsera f
**brake (n)** freno m
**brake fluid** líquido de freno
**brake light** luz de freno
**branch (office)** sucursal f
**brand** marca f
**brandy** brandy m
**bread** pan m
**break** romper
**breakable** se puede romper, frágil
**breakdown (of car)** avería f
**breakdown van** camion de reparación de averías
**breakfast** desayuno m
**break-in** robo m
**breast** pecho m, teta f
**breathe** respirar
**breeze** brisa f
**brewery** fábrica de cerveza
**brick** ladrillo m
**bride** novia f
**bridegroom** novio m
**bridge** puente m
**briefcase** maletín m
**bright** brillante
**bring** traer
**bring in** introducir

ENGLISH → SPANISH

**brochure** folleto m
**broken** roto/a
**bronchitis** bronquitis f
**brooch** broche m
**broom** escoba f
**brother** hermano m
**brother-in-law**
cuñado m
**brown** pardo/a, marrón
**bruise (n)** morado m
**brush** cepillo m
**Brussels** Bruselas
**bucket** balde, cubo m
**buffet car** coche
comedor
**buggy** cochecito de niño
**build** construir
**building** edificio m
**bulb (light)** lamparilla f
**bulb (plant)** bulbo m
**bumper**
guardabarros m
**bun** magdalena f
**bunch** manojo m
**bureau de change**
oficina de cambio
**burglar** ladrón/
ladrona m/f
**burglary** robo m
**burn** quemar
**burst** explotar
**bus** autobús m
**bus stop**
parada de autobús
**bush** arbusto m
**business** negocios mpl
**business trip**
viaje de negocios

**busy** ocupado/a
**but** pero
**butcher** carnicero/a m/f
**butter** mantequilla f
**butterfly** mariposa f
**button** botón m
**buy** comprar
**by** por
**bypass (road)**
desviación, carretera de
circunvalación

# C

**cab** taxi m
**cabbage** repollo m
**cabin** cabina f
**cable car** teleférico m
**cake** pastel m, tarta f
**cake shop** pastelería f
**calculator** calculadora f
**calf** ternera f
**call (n)** llamada f
**call (vb)** llamar
**calm** calma
**camp (vb)** acampar
**camp site**
campamento m
**can (n)** lata f
**can (vb)** poder
**can opener**
abridor de latas
**Canada** Canadá
**canal** canal m
**cancel** cancelar
**cancellation**
cancelación f
**cancer** cáncer m
**candle** vela f

**candy** dulce m
**canoe** canoa f
**cap** gorro m
**capital (city)** capital f
**capital (money)**
   capital m
**car** coche, carro, auto m
**car ferry** transbordador
   de coches
**car hire** alquiler de
   coches
**car insurance**
   seguro de coche
**car keys**
   llaves del coche
**car parts** partes del
   coche
**car wash** lavado de
   coches
**caravan** remolque m
**caravan site**
   campamento de
   remolques
**carburettor**
   carburador m
**card** carta f, tarjeta f
**cardboard** cartón m
**cardigan** rebeca f
**careful** cuidado
**caretaker** portero/a m/f
**carpenter**
   carpintero/a m/f
**carpet** alfombra f
**carriage** vagón m
**carrier bag** bolsa f
**carrot** zanahoria f
**carry** cargar
**carry-cot** cuna portable

**carton** caja f
**case** caso m
**cash** efectivo, dinero
   efectivo
**cash desk** caja f
**cash dispenser**
   cajero automático
**cash register** caja f
**cashier** cajero/a m/f
**cassette** cassette f
**castle** castillo m
**casualty department**
   urgencias
**cat** gato/a m/f
**catch** coger, agarrar
**cathedral** catedral f
**Catholic (adj, n)**
   católico/a m/f
**cauliflower** coliflor f
**cave** cueva f
**CD player** centro
   musical, toca discos
**ceiling** cielo raso
**celery** apio m
**cellar** bodega f
**cemetery** cementerio m
**Centigrade** centígrado
**centimetre**
   centímetro m
**central heating**
   calefacción central
**central locking**
   bloqueo automático
**centre** centro m
**century** siglo m
**certain** certeza
**certainly** ciertamente,
   claro

ENGLISH → SPANISH

93

ENGLISH → SPANISH

**certificate** certificado m
**chair** silla f
**chair lift** elevador
  de silla
**chambermaid**
  camarera f
**champagne** champán m
**change (n)** cambio m
**change (vb)** cambiar
**changing room**
  vestuario m
**channel** canal m
**chapel** capilla f
**charcoal** carbón m
**charge** cargar
**charge card**
  tarjeta de crédito
**charter flight**
  vuelo chárter
**cheap** barato/a
**cheap rate**
  precio barato
**cheaper** más barato
**check** registrar
**check in** registrarse,
  inscribirse
**cheek** mejilla f
**Cheers!** ¡Salud!
**cheese** queso m
**chef** cocinero/a m/f
**chemist**
  farmacéutico/a m/f
**cheque** cheque m
**cheque book**
  libreta de cheques
**cheque card** tarjeta de
  identidad bancario
**cherry** cereza f

**chess** ajedrez m
**chest** pecho m
**chest of drawers**
  cómoda f
**chestnut** castaño m
**chewing gum** goma de
  mascar, chicle m
**chicken** pollo m
**chicken pox** varicela f
**child** niño/a, chico/a,
  chaval/a m/f
**child car seat** asiento
  de coche para niños
**chimney** chimenea f
**chin** barbilla f, mentón m
**China** China
**china** porcelana f
**chips** patatas fritas,
  papas fritas fpl
**chives** cebolleta f
**chocolate** chocolate m
**chocolates**
  bombones mpl
**choir** coro m
**choose** escoger, elegir
**chop** cortar
**Christian name**
  nombre de pila
**Christmas** Navidad f
**Christmas Eve**
  Nochebuena f
**church** iglesia f
**cider** sidra f
**cigar** puro m
**cigarette** cigarrillo m
**cigarette lighter**
  mechero m,
  encendedor m

**cinema** cine m
**circle** círculo m
**cistern** cisterna f
**citizen** ciudadano/a m/f
**city** ciudad f
**city centre** centro de la ciudad
**class** clase f
**clean (adj)** limpio/a
**clean (vb)** limpiar
**cleaning solution** detergente m
**cleansing lotion** crema limpiadora
**clear (adj)** claro/a
**clever** listo/a, inteligente
**client** cliente m/f
**cliff** acantilado m
**climate** clima m
**climb** subir
**cling film** plástico para envolver
**clinic** clínica f
**cloakroom** baño m, servicios mpl
**clock** reloj m
**closed** cerrado/a
**cloth** paño m
**clothes** ropas fpl
**clothes line** tendedero m
**clothes peg** broches para la ropa, pinza f
**clothing** ropa f
**cloud** nube f
**clutch (car)** embrague m
**coach** autocar m

**coal** carbón m
**coast** costa f
**coastguard** guardia costera
**coat** abrigo m
**coat hanger** percha para abrigo
**cockroach** cucaracha f
**cocoa** cacao m
**coconut** coco m
**cod** bacalao m
**code** código m
**coffee** café m
**coil (n, contraceptive)** espiral f
**coil (n, rope)** rollo m
**coin** moneda f
**Coke** Coca Cola f
**colander** colador m
**cold** frío/a
**collapse (vb)** derrumbarse
**collar** cuello m
**collarbone** clavícula f
**colleague** colega m/f
**collect** recoger
**collect call** llamada a cobro revertido
**colour** color m
**colour blind** daltónico/a
**colour film** film a color
**comb (n)** peine m
**comb (vb)** peinar
**come** venir
**come back** volver, regresar
**come in** entre

**comedy** comedia f
**comfortable** cómodo/a
**company** compañía f
**compartment** compartimento m
**compass** compás m
**complain** quejarse
**complaint** queja f
**completely** completamente, totalmente
**composer** compositor/a m/f
**compulsory** obligatorio/a
**computer** ordenador m, computadora f
**concert** concierto m
**concession** concesión f
**concussion** conmoción cerebral
**condition** condición f
**condom** preservativo, condón m
**conference** conferencia f
**confirm** confirmar
**confirmation** confirmación f
**confused** confundido/a
**Congratulations!** ¡Enhorabuena! ¡Felicitaciones!
**connecting flight** vuelo de conexión
**connection (elec)** conexión f

**connection (phone)** instalación f
**conscious** conciente
**constipated** estreñido/a
**consulate** consulado m
**contact** contacto m
**contact lenses** lentes de contacto
**continue** continuar
**contraceptive** anticonceptivo m/f
**contract** contrato m
**convenient** conveniente
**cook (n)** cocinero/a m/f
**cook (vb)** cocinar
**cooker** cocina f, hornillo m
**cookie** galleta f
**cooking utensils** utensillos de cocina
**cool** fresco/a
**cool bag, cool box** nevera portátil
**copy** copiar
**cork** corcho m
**corkscrew** sacacorcho m
**corner** esquina f
**correct (adj)** correcto/a
**corridor** pasillo m
**cost** coste, costo m
**cot** cuna f
**cotton** algodón m
**cotton wool** algodón hidrófilo
**couch** sofá m
**couchette** litera f

**cough (n)** tos f
**cough (vb)** toser
**cough mixture** jarabe para la tos
**Could I?** ¿Podría? ¿Puedo?
**couldn't** no puedo
**counter** mostrador m
**country** país m
**countryside** campo m, afueras
**couple** pareja f
**courier service** servicio de entrega/courier
**course** curso m
**cousin** primo/a m/f
**cover charge** entrada f
**cow** vaca f
**crab** cangrejo m
**craft** artesanía f
**cramp** calambre m
**crash (vb)** chocar
**crash helmet** casco m
**crazy** loco/a
**cream** crema f
**crèche** guardería de niños
**credit card** tarjeta de crédito
**crime** delito m
**crisps** patatas fritas, papas fritas fpl
**crockery** loza f
**cross (n)** cruz m
**cross (vb)** cruzar
**crossing** cruce m
**crossroads** cruce de caminos

**crossword puzzle** crucigrama m
**crowd** muchedumbre f
**crowded** lleno/a, repleto/a
**crown** corona f
**cruise** crucero m
**crutches** muletas fpl
**cry** llorar
**cucumber** pepino m
**cufflinks** gemelos mpl
**cup** taza f, pocillo m
**cupboard** armario m, ropero m
**curly** rizado/a
**currency** moneda f
**current (n)** corriente f
**curtain** cortina f
**cushion** almohadón m
**custard** natillas fpl, crema pastelera
**custom** costumbre f
**customer** cliente m/f
**customs** aduana f
**cut** cortar
**cutlery** cubertería f
**cycle (vb)** montar/ andar en bicicleta
**cycle track** sendero de bicicletas
**cyst** quiste m
**cystitis** cistitis f
**Czech Republic** República Checa

**D**
**daily** diariamente
**damage** daño m

ENGLISH → SPANISH

97

**damp** humedad f
**dance (vb)** bailar
**danger** peligro m
**dangerous** peligroso/a
**dark** oscuro/a
**date (appointment)** cita f
**date (fruit)** dátil m
**date (of year)** fecha f
**date of birth** fecha de nacimiento
**daughter** hija f
**daughter-in-law** nuera f
**dawn (n)** alba f, amanecer m
**day** día m
**dead** muerto/a
**deaf** sordo/a
**deal** trato m
**dear** querido/a
**death** muerte f
**debts** deudas fpl
**decaffeinated** descafeinado/a
**December** diciembre m
**decide** decidir
**decision** decisión f
**deck chair** silla de patio, tumbona f
**deduct** descontar
**deep** profundo/a
**definitely** definitiva- mente, por supuesto
**degree (measure- ment)** grado
**degree (qualification)** título
**delay** demora f

**deliberately** deliberadamente
**delicious** delicioso/a, rico/a
**deliver** entregar
**delivery** entrega f
**Denmark** Dinamarca
**dental floss** hilo dental
**dentist** dentista m/f
**dentures** dentaduras
**depart** salir
**department** sección f
**department store** grandes almacenes mpl, tienda de departamentos
**departure** salida f
**departure lounge** sala de embarque
**deposit** depósito m
**describe** describir
**description** descripción f
**desert** desierto m
**desk** escritorio m
**dessert** postre m
**destination** destino m
**details** datos, detalles mpl
**detergent** detergente m
**detour** desvío m
**develop** desarrollar
**diabetic (adj, n)** diabético/a m/f
**dial (vb)** marcar
**dialling code** prefijo m

**dialling tone** señal de marcar
**diamond** diamante m
**diaper** pañal m
**diarrhoea** diarrea f
**diary** agenda f, diario m
**dice** dados mpl
**dictionary** diccionario m
**die** morir
**diesel** diesel m
**diet** dieta f
**difference** diferencia f
**different** diferente
**difficult** difícil
**dinghy** bote m, lancha neumática
**dining room** comedor m
**dinner** cena f
**direct (adj)** directo/a
**direction** dirección f
**dirty** sucio/a
**disabled** inválido/a
**disappear** desaparecer
**disappointed** decepcionado/a
**disaster** desastre m
**disconnected** desconectado
**discount** descuento m
**discover** descubrir
**disease** enfermedad f
**dish** plato m
**dishtowel** trapo de cocina
**dishwasher** lavaplatos m
**disinfectant** desinfectante m

**disk** disco m
**disposable diapers/ nappies** pañales descartables
**distance** distancia f
**district** barrio m, distrito m
**disturb** molestar
**dive** bucear
**diving board** trampolín m
**divorced** divorciado
**DIY shop** ferretería f
**dizzy** mareado/a
**do** hacer
**doctor** médico/a m/f
**document** documento m
**dog** perro/a m/f
**doll** muñeca f
**domestic** doméstico/a
**door** puerta f
**doorbell** timbre m
**doorman** portero m
**double** doble
**double bed** cama doble
**double room** habitación doble
**doughnut** donut m, rosquilla f
**downhill** cuesta abajo, barranca abajo
**downstairs** abajo
**dozen** docena f
**drain (n)** desagüe m
**draught** corriente f
**draught beer** cerveza de barril/tirada

**drawer** cajón m
**drawing** dibujo m
**dreadful** horrible
**dress** vestido m
**dressing (bandage)** vendaje m
**dressing (salad)** aliño m, vinagreta f
**dressing gown** bata f
**drill (n)** taladro m
**drink (n)** bebida f
**drink (vb)** beber
**drinking water** agua potable
**drive** conducir, manejar
**driver** conductor/a m/f, chófer m
**driving licence** carnet de conducir, licencia de conductor
**drop (n)** gota f
**drug (medicine)** medicamento m
**drug (narcotic)** droga f
**drunk (adj, n)** borracho/a m/f
**dry** seco/a
**dry cleaner's** tintorería f
**dryer** secadora f
**duck** pato/a m/f
**due** pagadero/a
**dull** apagado/a, pesado/a
**dummy** chupete m
**during** durante
**dust** polvo m
**dustbin** cubo de la basura
**duster** paño m, trapo m

**dustpan** recogedor m
**Dutch, Dutchman, Dutchwoman (adj, n)** holandés/holandesa m/f
**duty-free** libre de impuestos
**duvet** edredón m
**duvet cover** funda para edredón
**dye (n)** tinte m
**dye (vb)** teñir, colorear
**dynamo** dínamo f

**E**
**each** cada
**eagle** águila f
**ear** oído m
**earache** dolor de oídos
**earphones** auriculares mpl
**earrings** pendientes, aros mpl
**earth** tierra f
**earthquake** terremoto m
**east** este m
**Easter** Semana Santa
**Easter egg** huevo de pascua
**easy** fácil
**eat** comer
**EC** Comunidad Europea
**economy** economía f
**economy class** clase económica
**edge** borde m
**eel** anguila f
**egg** huevo m

**either ... or** o ... o
**elastic** elástico/a
**elbow** codo m
**electric** eléctrico/a
**electrician**
  electricista m/f
**electricity** electricidad f
**elevator** elevador,
  asecensor m
**embassy** embajada f
**emergency**
  emergencia f
**emergency exit** salida
  de emergencia
**empty** vacío/a
**end** final m
**engaged (occupied)**
  ocupado/a
**engaged (to be
  married)**
  comprometido/a
**engine** motor m
**engineer** ingeniero/a m/f
**England** Inglaterra
**English (language)**
  inglés
**English Channel** Canal
  de la Mancha
**English, Englishman/
  woman (adj, n)**
  inglés/inglesa m/f
**enjoy** disfrutar
**enlargement**
  ampliación f
**enough** suficiente
**enquiry** informe m,
  investigación f

**enquiry desk**
  mostrador de
  información
**enter** entrar
**entrance** entrada f
**entrance fee** entrada f
**envelope** sobre m
**epilepsy** epilepsia f
**epileptic** epiléptico/a
**equipment** equipo m
**error** error m
**escalator** escalera
  mecánica
**escape (vb)** escapar
**especially**
  especialmente
**essential** esencial
**estate agent** agente
  inmobiliario/a
**Estonia** Estonia
**EU** Unión Europea
**Europe** Europa
**European (adj, n)**
  europeo/a m/f
**even (adj)** parejo/a,
  uniforme
**even (adv)** hasta
**evening** tarde f, (early),
  noche f (late)
**eventually** finalmente
**every** cada
**everyone** cada uno,
  todos/todas m/f
**everything** todo
**everywhere** por todas
  partes
**exactly** exactamente
**examination** examen m

ENGLISH → SPANISH

ENGLISH → SPANISH

**example, for example**
ejemplo m, por ejemplo
**excellent** excelente
**except** excepto
**excess luggage**
exceso de equipaje
**exchange (n)** cambio,
intercambio m
**exciting** entusiasmante
**exclude** excluir
**excursion** excursión f
**excuse (n)** disculpa f
**Excuse me!** ¡Perdón!
**exhaust pipe** tubo
de escape
**exhausted** agotado/a
**exhibition** exposición f
**exit** salida f
**expect** esperar
**expenses** gastos mpl
**expensive** caro/a
**experienced**
con experiencia,
experimentado/a
**expire** caducar, vencer
**explain** explicar
**explosion** explosión f
**export** exportar
**exposure** exposición f,
revelación f
**express (train)**
expreso m
**extension** extensión f
**extension lead** cable
de extensión
**extra** extra
**extraordinary**
extraordinario/a

**eye** ojo m
**eye drops**
gotas para los ojos
**eye make-up remover**
desmaquillador para
ojos
**eye shadow** sombra
de ojos

**F**
**fabric** tejido m
**façade** fachada f
**face** cara f
**factory** fábrica f
**faint (vb)** desmayarse
**fair (fête)** feria f
**fair (hair colour)**
rubio/a
**fair (just)** justo/a
**fairly** bastante
**fake (adj)** falso/a
**fake (vb)** simular
**fall** caer
**false** falso/a
**family** familia f
**famous** famoso/a
**fan** ventilador m
**fanbelt** correa del
ventilador
**far (adj)** lejano/a
**far (adv)** lejos
**fare** tarifa f
**farm** granja f
**farmer** granjero/a m/f
**farmhouse** cortijo m,
hacienda f
**fashionable** de moda
**fast** rápido/a

**fasten** abrochar, ajustar
**fasten seatbelt**
  ajustar el cinturón
  de seguridad
**fat** gordo/a
**father** padre m
**father-in-law** suegro m
**fatty** graso/a
**fault** defecto m, culpa f
**faulty** defectuoso/a
**favourite** favorito/a
**fax** facsímil
**February** febrero m
**feed (vb)** alimentar
**feel** sentir
**feet** pies mpl
**female** mujer f
**fence** alambrada f
**fender** parachoques m,
  guardabarros m
**ferry** transbordador m,
  ferry m
**festival** festival m
**fetch** buscar, traer
**fever** fiebre f
**few, a few** pocos/as m/f
**fiancé, fiancée** novio/a,
  prometido/a m/f
**field** campo m
**fight (n)** pelea, lucha f
**fight (vb)** luchar, pelear
**file (folder)** archivo m,
  carpeta f
**file (tool)** lima f
**fill, fill in, fill up** llenar
**fillet** filete m
**filling (sandwich)**
  relleno m

**filling (tooth)**
  empaste m
**film (n)** película f
**film (vb)** filmar
**film processing**
  revelado
**filter** filtro m
**filthy** mugriento/a
**find** encontrar
**fine (adj)** fino/a
**fine (n)** multa f
**finger** dedo m
**finish (vb)** terminar
**fire** fuego m
**fire brigade**
  bomberos mpl
**fire exit** salida de
  emergencia
**fire extinguisher**
  extintor de fuego
**first, at first**
  primero/a, al principio
**first aid** primeros
  auxilios
**first-aid kit** maletín de
  primeros auxilios
**first class**
  primera clase
**first floor** primer piso m
**first name** primer
  nombre, nombre de pila
**fish** pescado m
**fishing permit**
  permiso de pesca
**fishing rod**
  caña de pescar
**fishmonger's**
  pescadería f

ENGLISH → SPANISH

**fit (healthy)** en forma
**fitting room** cambiador m
**fix** arreglar, reparar
**fizzy** con gas
**flannel** franela f
**flash (of lightning)** relámpago
**flashlight** linterna eléctrica
**flask** termo m
**flat (n)** apartamento m, piso m
**flat battery** batería descargada
**flat tyre** neumático sin aire
**flavour** sabor m
**flaw** desperfecto m, imperfección f
**flea** pulga f
**flight** vuelo m
**flip flops** chancletas fpl
**flippers** aletas fpl
**flood** inundación f
**floor (of room)** suelo m
**floor (storey)** piso m
**floorcloth** trapo/paño para el suelo
**florist** florista m/f
**flour** harina f
**flower** flor f
**flu** gripe f
**fluent** con fluidez
**fly (vb)** volar
**fog** niebla, neblina f
**folk** gente f
**follow** seguir

**food** alimento m, comida f
**food poisoning** comida envenenada
**food shop** almacén m, tienda f
**foot** pie m
**football** fútbol m
**football match** partido/juego de fútbol
**footpath** sendero m
**for** por, para
**forbidden** prohibido/a
**forehead** frente f
**foreign** raro/a
**foreign, foreigner (adj, n)** extranjero/a m/f
**forest** bosque m
**forget** olvidar
**fork** tenedor m
**form (document)** formulario m
**form (shape)** forma f
**formal** formal, educado/a
**fortnight** quincena f
**fortress** fuerte m
**fortunately** por suerte
**fountain** fuente f
**four-wheel drive** cuatro por cuatro
**fox** zorro/a m/f
**fracture** fractura f
**frame** marco m
**France** Francia
**free** libre
**freelance** por su cuenta, independiente
**freeway** autopista f

**freezer** congelador m
**French, Frenchman/woman (adj, n)** francés/francesa m/f
**French fries** patatas fritas, papas fritas fpl
**frequent** frecuente
**fresh** fresco/a
**Friday** viernes m
**fridge** nevera f, refrigerador m
**fried** frito/a
**friend** amigo/a m/f
**friendly** amigable, simpático/a
**frog** rana f
**from (origin)** de
**from (time)** desde
**front** frente m
**frost** helada f
**frozen** congelado/a
**fruit** fruta f
**fruit juice** zumo/jugo de fruta
**fry** freír
**frying pan** sartén f
**fuel** gasolina f, combustible m
**fuel gauge** indicador de la gasolina
**full** lleno/a
**full board** pensión completa
**fun (adj)** divertido/a
**fun (n)** diversión f
**funeral** funeral m
**funicular** funicular m
**funny** gracioso/a

**fur** piel f
**fur coat** abrigo de piel
**furnished** amueblado
**furniture** muebles mpl
**further** más allá
**fuse** fusible m
**fuse box** caja de fusibles
**future** futuro m

**G**
**Gallery** galería f
**gallon** galón m
**game** juego m
**garage** garaje m
**garden** jardín m
**garlic** ajo m
**gas** gas, combustible m
**gas cooker** hornalla f, estufilla f
**gate** puerta f
**gay** gay, homosexual
**gay bar** bar gay
**gear** equipo m, ropa f
**gear lever** palanca de cambios
**gearbox** caja de cambios
**general** general
**generous** generoso/a
**Geneva** Ginebra
**gents' toilet** servicio de caballeros, baño de hombres
**genuine** auténtico/a, genuino/a, real
**German (adj, n)** alemán, alemana m/f

ENGLISH → SPANISH

ENGLISH → SPANISH

**German measles** rubeola f
**Germany** Alemania
**get** obtener
**get off** bajar
**get on** subir
**get up** levantarse
**gift** regalo m
**girl** niña f
**girlfriend** novia f
**give** dar
**give back** devolver
**glacier** glaciar m
**glad** encantado/a
**glass (tumbler)** vaso m
**glasses (spectacles)** lentes m/f, gafas fpl, anteojos mpl
**gloomy** apagado/a
**gloves** guantes mpl
**glue** pegamento m
**go** ir
**go (by car)** ir/andar conducir, ir/andar manejar
**go (on foot)** andar
**go away** irse
**go back** volver
**goat** cabra f
**God** Dios m
**goggles** gafas protectoras
**gold** oro m
**golf club (place)** club de golf
**golf club (stick)** palo de golf

**golf course** campo de golf
**good** bueno/a
**good afternoon** buenas tardes
**good day** buenos días
**good evening** buenas tardes (if still light)
**Good Friday** Viernes Santo
**good luck** buena suerte
**good morning** buenos días
**good night** buenas noches
**goodbye** adiós
**goose** ganso m
**Gothic** gótico/a
**government** gobierno m
**gradually** poco a poco, gradualmente
**gram** gramo m
**grammar** gramática f
**grand** grandioso/a
**granddaughter** nieta f
**grandfather** abuelo m
**grandmother** abuela f
**grandparents** abuelos mpl
**grandson** nieto m
**grapes** uvas fpl
**grass** césped m
**grated** rallado/a
**grateful** agradecido/a
**gravy** salsa f
**greasy** graso/a
**great** gran, grande, vasto/a, importante

**Great Britain**
Gran Bretaña
**Greece** Grecia
**Greek (adj, n)**
griego/a m/f
**green** verde
**greengrocer's**
verdulería
**greeting** saludo m
**grey** gris
**grilled** a la parrilla
**ground** tierra f
**ground floor**
planta baja
**group** grupo m
**guarantee** garantía f
**guard** guardia m/f
**guest** huésped/a m/f
**guesthouse** pensión f
**guide** guía m/f
**guide book**
guía de turismo
**guided tour**
visita guiada
**guitar** guitarra f
**gun** arma f
**gym** gimnasio m

**H**
**hail** granizo m
**hair** cabello m, pelo m
**hairbrush**
cepillo de pelo
**haircut** corte de pelo
**hairdresser**
peluquero/a m/f
**hairdresser's**
peluquería f

**hairdryer** secador
de pelo
**half (adj)** medio/a,
**half (n)** mitad f
**hall** sala f
**ham** jamón m
**hamburger**
hamburguesa f
**hammer** martillo m
**hand** mano f
**hand luggage**
equipaje de mano
**handbag** bolso m,
cartera f
**handbrake**
freno de mano
**handicapped**
minusválido/a
**handkerchief** pañuelo m
**handle** mango m,
palanca f
**handmade**
hecho a mano
**handsome** guapo/a
**hang up (phone)**
colgar
**hanger** percha f
**hang-gliding** vuelo libre,
aladeltismo
**hangover** resaca f
**happen** pasar
**happy** feliz
**Happy Easter!**
¡Feliz Semana Santa!
**Happy New Year!**
¡Feliz Año Nuevo!
**harbour** puerto m
**hard** duro/a

ENGLISH → SPANISH

107

ENGLISH → SPANISH

**hard disk** disco duro
**hardly** apenas
**hardware shop**
   ferretería **f**
**harvest** cosecha **f**
**hat** sombrero **m**
**have** tener
**have to** deber,
   tener que
**hay fever**
   fiebre del heno
**hazelnut** avellana **f**
**he** él
**head** cabeza **f**
**headache**
   dolor de cabeza
**headlight/s** faro **m**,
   luces delanteras
**headphones**
   auriculares **mpl**
**health food shop**
   tienda de alimentos
   naturales
**healthy** saludable
**hear** oír, escuchar
**hearing aid** audífono **m**
**heart** corazón **m**
**heart attack**
   ataque al corazón
**heartburn** acedía **f**
**heat** calor **m**
**heater** calefactor **m**
**heating** calefacción **f**
**heavy** pesado/a
**heel** talón **m**
**height** altura **f**
**helicopter** helicóptero **m**
**helmet** casco **m**

**Help!** ¡Ayuda!
**help (vb)** ayudar
**hem** dobladillo **m**, orilla **f**
**her** su
**herbal tea** té de
   hierbas, té natural
**herbs** hierbas **fpl**
**here** aquí, acá
**hernia** hernia **f**
**hide** esconder
**high** alto/a
**high blood pressure**
   presión alta (sangre)
**high chair** silla alta
**him, to him** él, a él
**hip** cadera **f**
**hip replacement**
   reemplazo de cadera
**hire (vb)** alquilar
**hire car** coche de
   alquiler
**his** su
**historic** histórico/a
**history** historia **f**
**hit** golpear
**hitchhike** hacer
   autostop, hacer dedo
**hold** tener
**hole** hueco **m**, hoyo **m**,
   agujero **m**
**holidays** vacaciones **fpl**
**holy** sagrado/a
**home** casa **f**
**homesickness**
   echar de menos
**homosexual**
   homosexual
**honest** honrado/a

**honey** miel f
**honeymoon**
luna de miel
**hood (car)** capó/
capota m/f
**hood (garment)**
capucha f
**hope** esperanza f
**hopefully** ojalá
**horn (animal)** cuerno m
**horn (car)** bocina f
**horse** caballo m
**horse racing**
carrera de caballos
**horse riding**
paseo a caballo
**hose pipe** manguera f
**hospital** hospital m
**hospitality** hospitalidad f
**hostel** parador m,
albergue m
**hot** caliente
**hot spring** termas fpl
**hot-water bottle**
bolsa de agua caliente
**hour** hora f
**hourly (adj)** cada hora
**hourly (adv)** por horas
**house** casa f
**house wine**
vino de la casa
**housework** trabajo
doméstico, tarea f
**hovercraft**
hidrodeslizador m
**How?** ¿Cómo?
**How are you?**
¿Cómo estás?

**How do you do?**
¿Qué tal? ¿Cómo
estás?
**How many?**
¿Cuánto/a?
**How much is it?**
¿Cuánto es?
**humid** húmedo/a
**humour** humor m
**Hungarian (adj, n)**
húngaro/a m/f
**Hungary** Hungría
**hungry** con hambre
**hunt** cazar
**hunting permit**
permiso de caza
**hurry (vb)** darse prisa
**hurt (vb)** doler
**hurts** duele
**husband** marido,
esposo m
**hydrofoil** hidroala f
**hypodermic needle**
aguja hipodérmica

**I**
**I** yo
**ice** hielo m
**ice cream** helado m
**ice rink** pista de hielo
**ice skates** patines mpl
**iced coffee** café
helado m
**idea** idea f
**identity card** carné de
identidad, tarjeta de
identidad, documento
de identidad

ENGLISH → SPANISH

**if** si
**if not** si no
**ignition** encendido m
**ignition key**
  llave de contacto, llave
  de encendido
**ill** enfermo/a
**illness** enfermedad f
**immediately**
  inmediatamente
**important** importante
**impossible** imposible
**improve** mejorar
**in** en
**inch** pulgada f
**included** incluido
**inconvenience**
  inconveniente f
**incredible** increíble
**Indian (adj, n)**
  indio/a m/f
**indicator** indicador
  de giro, intermitente m
**indigestion** indigestión f
**indoor pool** piscina
  climatizada/cubierta
**indoors** a puertas
  adentro
**infection** infección f
**infectious** infeccioso/a
**inflammation**
  inflamación f
**inflate** inflar
**informal** informal
**information**
  información f
**ingredients**
  ingredientes mpl

**injection** inyección f
**injured** lastimado/a,
  herido/a
**injury** herida f
**ink** tinta f
**in-laws** suegros mpl
**inn** posada f
**inner tube** tubo interno,
  cámara de aire
**insect** insecto m
**insect bite**
  picadura de insecto
**insect repellent**
  repelente de insectos
**inside** dentro, adentro
**insist** insistir
**insomnia** insomnio m
**inspect** registrar
**instant coffee**
  café instantáneo
**instead** en lugar de
**insulin** insulina f
**insurance** seguro m
**intelligent** inteligente
**intend** significar
**interesting** interesante
**international**
  internacional
**interpreter**
  intérprete m/f
**intersection** cruce m
**interval** intervalo m
**into** en
**introduce** introducir,
  presentar (people)
**investigation**
  investigación f
**invitation** invitación f

**invite** invitar
**invoice** factura f
**Ireland** Irlanda
**Irish, Irishman/woman (adj, n)** irlandés/irlandesa m/f
**iron (n, appliance)** plancha f
**iron (n, metal)** hierro m
**iron (vb)** planchar
**ironing board** tabla de planchar
**ironmonger's** ferretería f
**is** es/está
**island** isla f
**it (direct object)** lo/la
**it (indirect object)** le
**it (subject)** él/ella/ello
**Italian (adj, n)** italiano/a m/f
**Italian (language)** italiano
**Italy** Italia
**itch (n)** picor m
**itch (vb)** picar

**J**
**jack (car)** gato m
**jacket** chaqueta f, abrigo m
**jam** jalea f, mermelada f
**jammed** tapado
**January** enero m
**jar** frasco m
**jaundice** ictericia f
**jaw** mandíbula f
**jealous** celoso/a

**jelly** jalea f
**jellyfish** medusa, aguamala f
**jersey** jersey m
**Jew, Jewish (n, adj)** judío/a m/f
**jeweller's** joyería f
**jewellery** joyas fpl
**job** trabajo m
**jog (n)** trote m
**jog (vb)** correr, trotar
**join** unirse, asociarse
**joint** juntura f
**joke** broma f
**journey** travesía f, viaje m
**joy** alegría f
**judge** juez m/f
**jug** jarra f
**juice** zumo m, jugo m
**July** julio m
**jump (n)** salto m
**jump (vb)** saltar
**jump leads** cables de conexion de batería
**jumper** súeter, jersey m
**junction** cruce m
**June** junio m
**just (fair)** justo/a
**just (only)** solamente

**K**
**keep** guardar
**Keep the change!** ¡Guarde el cambio!
**kettle** hervidor m
**key** llave f
**key ring** llavero m
**kick** patear

ENGLISH → SPANISH

111

**kidney** riñón m
**kill** matar
**kilo** kilo m
**kilogram** kilogramo m
**kilometre** kilómetro m
**kind** amable
**king** rey m
**kiosk** quiosko m
**kiss (n)** beso m
**kiss (vb)** besar
**kitchen** cocina f
**kitchenette** cocinilla f
**knee** rodilla f
**knickers** bragas fpl
**knife** cuchillo m
**knit** tejer
**knitting needle**
   aguja de tejer
**knitwear** tejido m
**knock** golpear
**knock down** derribar
**knock over** atropellar
**know** saber, conocer

**L**
**label** etiqueta f
**lace** puntilla f
**ladder** escalera f
**ladies' toilet**
   servicio de damas,
   baño de mujeres
**ladies' wear**
   ropa de mujer
**lady** dama f, mujer f,
   señora f
**lager** cerveza rubia
**lake** lago m
**lamb** cordero m

**lamp** lámpara f
**land** tierra f
**landlady** propietaria f
**landlord** propietario m
**landslide**
   desprendimiento
   de tierras
**lane** carril m
**language** lengua f,
   idioma m
**language course**
   curso de idioma
**large** gran, grande
**last** último/a
**last night** anoche
**late** tarde
**later** luego, más tarde
**Latvia** Latvia
**laugh (n)** risa f
**laugh (vb)** reír
**launderette,**
   **laundromat**
   lavandería automática
**laundry** lavandería f
**lavatory** servicios mpl,
   baño m
**law** ley f
**lawyer** abogado/a m/f
**laxative (adj, n)**
   laxante m
**lazy** perezoso/a, vago/a
**lead (n, metal)** plomo
**lead (vb)** llevar
**lead-free** sin plomo
**leaf** hoja f
**leaflet** folleto m
**leak (n)** agujero m
**leak (vb)** gotear

**learn** aprender
**lease (n)** contrato de alquiler
**lease (vb)** arrendar
**leather** piel f, cuero m
**leave** salir, dejar
**leek** puerro m
**left, to the left** izquierdo/a, a la izquierda
**left-hand drive** conducción a la izquierda
**left-handed** zurdo/a
**leg** pierna f
**lemon** limón m
**lemonade** limonada f
**lend** prestar
**lens** lente f
**lenses** lentes m/f
**lentil** lenteja f
**lesbian (adj, n)** lesbiana f
**less** menos
**lesson** lección f, clase f
**let (vb, allow)** dejar, permitir
**let (vb, hire)** alquilar
**letter** carta f
**letterbox** buzón m
**lettuce** lechuga f
**level crossing** cruce a nivel
**lever** palanca f
**library** biblioteca f
**licence** licencia f, permiso m
**lid** tapa f

**lie (n, untruth)** mentira f
**lie (vb, fib)** mentir
**lie down** acostarse
**life** vida f
**life belt** cinturón salvavidas
**life insurance** seguro de vida
**life jacket** chaleco salvavidas
**lifeguard** socorrista m/f
**lift (n, elevator)** elevador, ascensor m
**lift (vb)** levantar
**light (adj, colour)** claro/a
**light (adj, weight)** ligero/a, liviano/a
**light (n)** luz f
**light (vb)** iluminar
**light bulb** bombilla f, lamparilla f
**lightning** rayo m
**like (prep)** como
**like (vb)** gustar
**lime** lima f
**line** línea f
**linen** lino m
**lingerie** ropa interior
**lion** león m
**lipstick** lápiz de labios
**liqueur** licor m
**list** lista f
**listen** escuchar
**Lithuania** Lituania
**litre** litro m
**litter (n)** basura f
**litter (vb)** ensuciar

**little** pequeño/a
**live** vivir
**lively** vivo/a
**liver** hígado m
**living room** sala de estar
**loaf** barra f
**lobby** vestíbulo m
**lobster** langosta f
**local** local
**lock (n)** cerradura f
**lock (vb)** cerrar
**lock in** guardar en el armario
**lock out** cerrar, dejar encerrado
**locked in** bajo llave
**locker** armario m
**lollipop** pirulí, chupón
**long (adj, size)** largo/a
**long (adj, time)** mucho/a
**long-distance call** llamada de larga distancia
**look after** cuidar
**look at** mirar
**look for** buscar
**look forward to** esperar con ilusión
**loose** suelto/a
**lorry** camioneta f
**lose** perder
**lost** perdido/a
**lost property** propiedad perdida
**lot** mucho/a
**loud** ruidoso/a

**lounge** sala de estar, salón m
**love (n)** amor m
**love (vb)** amar
**lovely** precioso/a
**low** bajo/a
**low fat** bajas calorías
**luck** suerte f
**luggage** equipaje m
**luggage rack** portaequipaje m
**luggage tag** etiqueta f
**luggage trolley** carrito para equipaje
**lump** terrón m, trozo m
**lunch** almuerzo m
**lung** pulmón m
**Luxembourg** Luxemburgo
**luxury** lujo m

**M**
**machine** máquina f
**mad** loco/a
**made** hecho/a
**magazine** revista f
**maggot** gusano m
**magnet** imán m
**magnifying glass** lupa f
**maid** criada f
**maiden name** nombre de soltera
**mail (n)** correo m
**mail (vb)** enviar por correo
**main** principal
**main course** plato principal

ENGLISH → SPANISH

**main post office**
correo central
**main road**
calle principal/mayor
**mains switch**
interruptor principal
**make** hacer
**male** masculino
**man** hombre m
**man-made fibre**
fibra sintética
**manager** gerente m/f
**manual (adj, n)**
manual m
**many** muchos/as
**map** mapa m
**marble** mármol m
**March** marzo m
**market** mercado m
**marmalade** mermelada f
**married** casado/a
**marsh** pantano m
**mascara** rímel m
**mashed potatoes**
puré de patatas/papas
**mask** máscara f
**Mass (rel)** misa f
**mast** mástil m
**match (sport)** partido m
**matches (for lighting)**
fósforos mpl
**material** tejido m
**matter** asunto m
**matter – it doesn't
matter** no importa
**mattress** colchón f
**May** mayo m
**may** poder

**maybe** quizás, tal vez
**mayonnaise** mayonesa f
**me** me
**meal** comida f
**mean (intend)** significar
**mean (nasty)** malo/a
**measles** sarampión m
**measure (n)** medida f
**measure (vb)** medir
**meat** carne f
**mechanic**
mecánico/a m/f
**medical insurance**
seguro médico
**medicine (drug)**
medicamento m
**medicine (science)**
medicina f
**medieval** medieval
**Mediterranean**
mediterráneo/a
**medium** mediano/a
**medium dry wine**
vino medio seco
**medium rare (meat)**
carne medio hecha
**medium sized**
talla media
**meet** encontrar
**meeting** reunión f
**melon** melón m
**melt** derretir
**men** hombres
**mend** remendar
**meningitis** meningitis
**menswear**
ropa de hombre
**mention** mencionar

ENGLISH → SPANISH

**menu** menú m
**meringue** merengue m
**message** recado m
**metal** metal m
**meter** contador m
**metre** metro m
**metro** metro m
**microwave oven**
  micro ondas m
**midday** mediodía m
**middle** medio m
**midnight** medianoche f
**might (vb)** poder
**migraine** migraña f
**mile** milla f
**milk** leche f
**minced meat**
  carne picada
**mind** mente f
**mineral water**
  agua mineral
**minister** ministro/a m/f
**mint** menta f
**minute** minuto m
**mirror** espejo m
**Miss** señorita f
**missing** perdido/a,
  desaparecido/a
**mist** neblina f
**mistake** error m
**misunderstanding**
  malentendido m
**mix (vb)** mezclar
**mix-up (n)** confusión f
**mix up (vb)** confundir
**mobile phone**
  teléfono móvil

**moisturizer**
  crema hidratante
**moment** momento m
**monastery** monasterio m
**Monday** lunes m
**money** dinero m
**money belt** monedero m
**money order** giro m
**month** mes m
**monthly** mensualmente
**monument**
  monumento m
**moon** luna f
**mooring** amarradero m
**more** más
**morning** mañana f
**mosque** mezquita f
**mosquito** mosquito m
**most** la mayoría de
**mostly** generalmente
**moth** polilla f
**mother** madre f
**mother-in-law** suegra f
**motor** motor m
**motorbike** motocicleta f
**motorboat** lancha f
**motorway** autopista f
**mountain** montaña f
**mountain rescue**
  rescate de montaña
**mountaineering**
  montañismo m
**mouse** ratón m
**moustache** bigote m
**mouth** boca f
**mouth ulcer**
  úlcera de boca

116

**mouthwash**
desinfectante bucal
**move** mover,
**move house** mudarse
de casa
**Mr** señor m
**Mrs** señora f
**Ms** señorita f
**much** mucho/a
**mud** lodo, barro m
**mug** tazón m
**mugged** robado
**mumps** paperas fpl
**muscle** músculo m
**museum** museo m
**mushroom** hongo m,,
champiñon m
**musician** músico/a m/f
**Muslim** musulmán/
musulmana m/f
**mussel** mejillón m
**must** deber
**mustard** mostaza f
**mutton** cordero m
**my** mi
**myself** yo mismo

# N
**nail** uña f
**nail brush** cepillo
de uñas
**nail file** lima de uñas
**nail polish/varnish**
pintura de uñas, esmalte
de uñas
**nail polish remover**
quitaesmalte

**nail scissors**
tijeras para uñas
**name** nombre m
**nanny** niñera f
**napkin** servilleta f
**nappy** pañal m
**narrow** angosto/a,
estrecho/a
**nasty** malo/a, sucio/a,
indecente
**national** nacional
**nationality** nacionalidad f
**natural** natural
**nature** naturaleza f
**nature reserve**
reserva natural
**nausea** náusea f
**navy** armada f
**navy blue** azul marino
**near (adj)** cercano/a
**near (adv)** cerca
**nearby (adj)** cercano/a
**nearby (adv)** cerca, en
los alrededores
**nearly** casi
**necessary** necesario/a
**neck** cuello m
**necklace** collar m
**need (n)** necesidad f
**need (vb)** necesitar
**needle** aguja f
**negative (n, photo)**
negativo m
**neighbour** vecino/a m/f
**neither ... nor** ni ... ni
**nephew** sobrino m
**nest** nido m
**net** red f

ENGLISH → SPANISH

**Netherlands** Países Bajos
**never** nunca
**new** nuevo/a
**New Year** Año Nuevo
**New Year's Eve** Nochevieja f
**New Zealand, New Zealander** Nueva Zelanda, neocelandés
**news** noticias fpl
**news stand** quiosko m
**newspaper** periódico m
**next** próximo/a
**nice** agradable
**niece** sobrina f
**night, last night** noche f, anoche
**nightdress** vestido de noche
**no** no
**nobody** nadie
**noise** ruido m
**noisy** ruidoso/a
**non-alcoholic** sin alcohol
**non-smoking** no fumador/a
**none** ninguno/a
**north** norte m
**North Sea** Mar del Norte
**Northern Ireland** Irlanda del Norte
**Norway** Noruega
**Norwegian (adj, n)** noruego/a m/f
**nose** nariz f

**not** no
**note** nota f
**notebook** cuaderno m
**notepaper** papel de carta
**nothing** nada
**nothing else** nada más
**noticeboard** tablón de anuncios
**novel** novela f
**November** noviembre m
**now** ahora
**nudist beach** playa nudista
**number** número m
**number plate** matrícula f
**nurse** enfermero/a m/f
**nursery (plants)** vivero m
**nursery school** guardería infantil, jardín de infancia
**nursery slope** pistas para principiantes
**nut** nuez f
**nut (for bolt)** tornillo m

**O**
**oak** roble m
**oar** remo m
**oats** avena f
**obtain** obtener
**occasionally** de vez en cuando
**occupation** ocupación f
**occupied (e.g. toilet)** ocupado/a

**ocean** océano m
**October** octubre m
**odd (number)** impar
**odd (strange)** raro/a
**of** de
**off** de
**office** oficina f
**often** con frecuencia
**oil** aceite m
**ointment** pomada f
**OK** bien, vale
**old** viejo/a
**old-age pensioner**
  jubilado/a m/f
**old-fashioned**
  pasado/a de moda
**olive** aceituna f
**olive oil** aceite de oliva
**omelette** tortilla f
**on** en, sobre
**once** una vez
**one** uno m
**one-way street**
  calle de una sola mano
**onion** cebolla f
**only (adj)** solamente
**only (adv)** sólo
**open** abierto/a
**open ticket** billete
  abierto
**opening times** horario
  de apertura
**opera** ópera f
**operation** operación f
**operator (phone)**
  operador/a m/f
**ophthalmologist**
  oculista m/f

**opposite** opuesto/a
**optician** óptico/a m/f
**or** o
**orange** naranja f
**orange juice**
  zumo/jugo de naranja
**orchestra** orquesta f
**order (n)** orden m
**order (vb)** pedir
**organic vegetables**
  verduras orgánicas
**other** otro/a
**otherwise** de otra
  forma, si no
**our** nuestro/a
**out** fuera, afuera
**out of order**
  no funciona
**outdoors** al aire libre
**outside** fuera, afuera
**outskirts** afueras
**oven** horno m
**ovenproof** resistente
  al horno, refractario/a
**over** sobre
**over here** acá, aquí
**over there** allá
**overcharge** cobrar
  excesivamente
**overcoat** abrigo m
**overdone** muy hecho
**overheat** recalentar
**overnight** por la noche,
  durante la noche
**overtake** adelantar
**owe** deber
**owl** lechuza f

ENGLISH → SPANISH

**owner** propietario/a, dueño/a **m/f**

**P**
**pacemaker** marcapasos **m**
**pacifier** chupete **m**
**pack (vb)** empacar
**package** paquete **m**
**package holiday** vacaciones organizadas
**packet** paquete **m**
**padlock** candado **m**
**page** página **f**
**paid** pagado/a
**pail** cubo **m**
**pain** dolor **m**
**painful** doloroso/a
**painkiller** mitigador, droga mitigadora, analgésico **m**
**paint (vb)** pintar
**paint (n)** pintura **f**
**painting** cuadro **m**
**pair** par **m**
**palace** palacio **m**
**pale** pálido/a
**pan** cacerola **f**
**pancake** crepe **f**
**panties** bragas **fpl**
**pants** pantalones **mpl**
**pantyhose** panty **m**
**paper** papel **m**
**paper napkins** servilletas de papel
**parcel** paquete **m**
**Pardon?** ¿Qué? ¿Disculpa?

**parents** padres **mpl**
**parents-in-law** suegros **mpl**
**park (n)** parque **m**
**park (vb)** aparcar
**parking disc** disco de aparcamiento
**parking meter** parquímetro **m**
**parking ticket** boleto de estacionamiento
**part** parte **f**
**partner (companion)** compañero/a **m/f**
**partner (business)** socio/a **m/f**
**party (celebration)** fiesta **f**
**party (political)** partido **m**
**pass (vb)** pasar
**pass control** control de pasaporte
**passenger** pasajero/a **m/f**
**passport** pasaporte **m**
**past** pasado **m**
**pastry** pastel **m**
**path** sendero **m**
**patient (adj, n)** paciente **m/f**
**pattern** patrón **m**
**pavement** calzada **f**
**pay** pagar
**payment** pago **m**
**payphone** teléfono pago/público

**pea** guisante m, chícharo m

**peach** melocotón m

**peak** pico m

**peak rate** precio de temporada alta

**peanut** cacahuete m, maní m

**pear** pera f

**pearl** perla f

**peculiar** peculiar

**pedal** pedal m

**pedestrian** peatón m

**pedestrian crossing** paso de peatones

**peel (n)** piel f

**peel (vb)** pelar

**peg** clavija f

**pen** lapicera, boli m

**pencil** lápiz m

**penfriend** amigo/a invisible, amigo/a por carta

**peninsula** península f

**people** gente f

**pepper (vegetable)** pimiento m

**pepper (spice)** pimienta f

**per** por

**perfect** perfecto/a

**performance** representación f

**perfume** perfume m

**perhaps** quizás, tal vez

**period** período m

**perm** permanente f

**permit (n)** permiso m

**permit (vb)** permitir

**person** persona f

**pet** animal doméstico

**petrol** combustible m, gasolina f

**petrol can** contenedor de gasolina

**petrol station** estación de servicio, gasolinera f

**pharmacist** farmacéutico/a m/f

**pharmacy** farmacia f

**phone** teléfono m

**phone booth** cabina telefónica

**phone card** tarjeta de llamadas

**phone number** número de teléfono

**photo** foto f

**photocopy (n)** fotocopia f

**photograph (n)** fotografía f

**photograph (vb)** fotografiar

**phrase book** libro de frases

**piano** piano m

**pickpocket** carterista f, ratero/a m/f

**picnic** picnic m, comida de campo

**picture** foto f

**picture frame** marco de foto

**pie** pastel m, empanada f

**piece** pieza f, pedazo m

ENGLISH → SPANISH

ENGLISH → SPANISH

**pig** cerdo m, puerco m/f
**pill** pastilla f
**pillow** almohada f
**pillowcase** funda para almohada
**pilot** piloto m
**pin** alfiler m
**pin number** número de clave
**pineapple** piña f, ananá m
**pink** rosa m
**pipe (plumbing)** cañería f
**pipe (smoking)** pipa f
**pity, It's a pity!** pena f, ¡Qué pena!
**place** lugar m
**plain** simple
**plait** trenza f
**plane** avión m
**plant** planta f
**plaster** escayola f, yeso m
**plastic** plástico/a
**plastic bag** bolsa de plástico
**plate** plato m
**platform** plataforma f, andén m
**play (n, theatre)** obra f
**play (vb, game)** jugar
**playground** patio de recreo
**please** por favor
**pleased** encantado/a
**Pleased to meet you!** ¡Encantado!

**plenty** suficiente demasiado
**pliers** alicates mpl
**plug (bath)** tapón m
**plug (elec)** enchufe m
**plum** ciruela f
**plumber** plomero/a, fontanero/a m/f
**p.m. (after noon)** por la tarde
**poached** escalfado
**pocket** bolsillo m
**point (n)** punto m
**point (vb)** señalar
**points (car)** platinos mpl
**poison** veneno m
**poisonous** venenoso/a
**Poland** Polonia
**Pole, Polish (n, adj)** polaco/a m/f
**police** policía f
**police station** estación de policía, comisaría f
**policeman/woman** agente de policía
**polish (n)** cera f
**polish (vb)** pulir
**polite** respetuoso/a, educado/a
**polluted** contaminado
**pool** piscina f
**poor (impecunious)** pobre
**poor (quality)** malo/a
**poppy** amapola f
**popular** popular
**population** población f

**pork** carne de cerdo, carne de puerco
**port (n, harbour)** puerto m
**port (n, wine)** oporto m
**porter** portero/a m/f
**portion** porción, parte f
**portrait** retrato m
**Portugal** Portugal
**Portuguese (adj, n)** portugués/ portuguesa m/f
**posh** elegante
**possible** posible
**post (n)** correo m
**post (vb)** enviar por correo
**post office** oficina de correos
**post office box** casilla de correo
**postage** franqueo m
**postage stamp** sello m, estampilla f
**postal code** código postal
**postbox** buzón m
**postcard** postal f
**poster** póster m
**postman/postwoman** cartero/a m/f
**postpone** aplazar
**potato** patata, papa f
**pothole** bache m
**pottery** cerámica f
**pound** libra f
**pour** servir
**powder** polvo m

**powdered milk** leche en polvo
**power cut** corte de electricidad
**practice** práctica f
**practise** practicar
**pram** cochecito m
**prawn** gamba f
**pray** rezar
**prefer** preferir
**pregnant** embarazada
**prescription** receta f
**present (adj)** presente
**present (n)** regalo m
**present (vb)** regalar
**pressure** presión f
**pretty** bonito/a
**price** precio m
**priest** cura m
**prime minister** primer/a ministro/a m/f
**print (vb)** imprimir
**printed matter** asunto escrito, impresos mpl
**prison** cárcel f
**private** privado/a
**prize** premio m
**probably** probablemente
**problem** problema m
**programme, program** programa m
**prohibited** prohibido/a
**promise (n)** promesa f
**promise (vb)** prometer
**pronounce** pronunciar
**properly** correctamente
**Protestant** protestante m/f

ENGLISH → SPANISH

**public** público/a
**public holiday** día
 feriado, fiesta nacional
**pudding** postre m
**pull** tirar
**pullover** jersey m,
 chaleco m
**pump (vb)** inflar
**puncture** pinchazo m
**puppet show**
 espectáculo de
 marionetas
**purple** morado/a
**purse** bolso m,
 monedero m
**push** empujar
**pushchair** silla de ruedas
**put** poner
**put up with** aguantar
**pyjamas** pijamas m

**Q**
**quality** calidad f
**quantity** cantidad f
**quarantine**
 cuarentena f
**quarrel (n)** riña f
**quarrel (vb)** pelear,
 discutir
**quarter** cuarto m
**quay** muelle m
**queen** reina f
**question** pregunta f,
 cuestión f
**queue (n)** cola f
**queue (vb)** hacer cola
**quickly** rápidamente
**quiet** tranquilo/a, quieto

**quilt** cobertor, edredón
**quite** completamente

**R**
**rabbit** conejo/a m/f
**rabies** rabia f
**race (people)** raza f
**race (sport)** carrera f
**race course**
 hipódromo m
**racket** raqueta f
**radiator** radiador m
**radio** radio f
**radish** rábano m
**rag** trapo m
**railway** ferrocarril m
**railway station**
 estación de tren,
 estación de ferrocarril
**rain** lluvia f
**raincoat** impermeable m
**raisin** pasa f
**rake** rastrillo m
**rape (n)** violación f
**rape (vb)** violar
**rare** raro/a
**rash** erupción m
**raspberry** frambuesa f
**rat** rata f
**rate (of exchange)**
 tipo de cambio
**raw** crudo/a
**razor** navaja de afeitar
**razor blade**
 hoja de afeitar
**read** leer
**ready** listo/a
**real** real

ENGLISH → SPANISH

**realize** darse cuenta
**really** realmente
**rear-view mirror**
  espejo retrovisor
**reasonable** razonable
**receipt** recibo m
**receiver (tax)**
  recaudador/a m/f
**receiver (telephone)**
  auricular m
**recently** recientemente
**reception** recepción f
**receptionist**
  recepcionista m/f
**recharge** recargar
**recipe** receta f
**recognize** reconocer
**recommend**
  recomendar
**record (n, legal)**
  documento m
**record (n, music)**
  disco m
**red** rojo/a
**red wine** vino tinto
**redcurrant** grosella roja
**reduce** reducir
**reduction** reducción f
**refund (n)**
  reembolso m
**refund (vb)** devolver,
  reembolsar
**refuse (n)** basura f
**refuse (vb)** rechazar
**region** región f
**register (n)** registro m
**register (vb)** certificar

**registered mail**
  correo certificado
**registration form**
  formulario de inscripción
**registration number**
  número de inscripción
**relative, relation**
  pariente m/f
**remain** quedarse
**remember** recordar
**rent (vb)** alquilar
**repair (n)** reparación f
**repair (vb)** reparar
**repeat** repetir
**reply (n)** respuesta f
**reply (vb)** contestar
**report (n)** informe m
**report (vb)** informar
**request (n)** petición f,
  pedido m, solicitud f
**request (vb)** pedir
**require** requerir
**rescue (n)** rescate m
**rescue** salvar
**reservation** reserva f
**reserve** reservar
**resident (adj, n)**
  residente m/f
**resort** complejo turístico
**rest (relax)** descansar
**rest (remainder)**
  resto m
**retired** jubilado/a,
  retirado/a
**return** regresar, volver
**return ticket** billete de
  ida y vuelta
**reverse (n)** revés m

ENGLISH → SPANISH

**reverse (vb)** dar
    marcha atrás
**reverse gear**
    marcha atrás
**reverse-charge call**
    llamada a cobro
    revertido
**revolting** asqueroso/a
**rheumatism** reuma m
**rib** costilla f
**ribbon** cinta f
**rice** arroz m
**rich** rico/a
**ride** montar
**ridiculous** ridículo/a
**right** derecho/a
**right-hand drive**
    conducción a la derecha
**ring (n)** anillo m
**ring (vb)** sonar
**ring road** camino
    circular
**rip-off** estafa f
**ripe** maduro/a
**river** río m
**road** calle f, camino m,
    carretera f
**road accident**
    accidente de tráfico
**road map** mapa de
    carreteras
**road sign** señal de tráfico
**road works** carretera
    en obras
**roll** darse vuelta
**roof** techo m
**roof-rack**
    portaequipaje m

**room** cuarto m,
    habitación f
**rope** soga, cuerda f
**rose (flower)** rosa f
**rotten** podrido/a
**rough** áspero/a
**roughly**
    aproximadamente
**round** redondo/a
**roundabout** rotonda f
**row (n)** fila f
**row (vb)** remar
**royal** real
**rubber** caucho m,
    goma f
**rubbish** basura f
**rubella** rubeola f
**rudder** timón m
**rug** alfombra f
**ruin** ruina f
**ruler (for measuring)**
    regla f
**rum** ron m
**run** correr
**rush** darse prisa
**rusty** oxidado/a
**rye bread**
    pan de centeno

**S**
**sad** triste
**saddle** silla de montar
**safe (adj)** seguro
**safe (n)** caja fuerte
**safety belt**
    cinturón de seguridad
**safety pin** imperdible m
**sail** navegar

**sailing** navegación f
**salad** ensalada f
**salad dressing**
  condimento para
  ensalada, vinagreta f
**sale** rebajas fpl
**sales representative**
  representante de ventas
**salesperson**
  vendedor/a m/f
**salmon** salmón m
**salt** sal f
**same** mismo/a, igual
**sand** arena f
**sandals** sandalias,
  ojotas fpl
**sandwich** bocadillo m,
  sandwich m
**sanitary pads**
  compresa higiénica
**Saturday** sábado m
**sauce** salsa f
**saucer** platillo m
**sausage** salchicha f
**save** ahorrar
**savoury** salado/a
**say** decir
**scales** balanza f
**scarf** bufanda f
**scenery** paisaje m
**school** escuela f
**scissors** tijeras fpl
**Scot, Scottish (n, adj)**
  escocés/escocesa m/f
**Scotland** Escocia
**scrambled eggs**
  huevos revueltos
**scratch (n)** arañazo m

**scratch (vb)** rascar
**screen** pantalla f
**screw** tornillo m
**screwdriver**
  destornillador m
**scrubbing brush**
  cepillo para fregar
**scuba diving**
  submarinismo m
**sea** mar m/f
**seagull** gaviota f
**seasick** mareado/a
**seaside** costa f
**season** temporada f
**season ticket** abono m,
  billete de temporada
**seasoning**
  condimento m
**seat** asiento m
**seatbelt** cinturón de
  seguridad
**seaweed** alga f
**secluded** aislado/a
**second** segundo/a
**second-class**
  segunda clase
**second-hand**
  segunda mano
**secretary**
  secretario/a m/f
**security guard**
  guardia de seguridad
**see** ver
**self-catering**
  alojamiento con cocina
**self-employed** trabajar
  por cuenta propia

ENGLISH → SPANISH

**ENGLISH → SPANISH**

**self-service** autoservicio m

**sell** vender

**sell-by date** fecha de vencimiento

**send** enviar

**senior citizen** jubilado/a m/f

**sentence (grammar)** frase f

**sentence (law)** sentencia f

**separate** separado/a

**September** septiembre m

**septic** séptico/a

**septic tank** tanque séptico

**serious** serio/a

**service** servicio m

**service charge** propina f

**serviette** servilleta f

**set menu** menú fijo

**several** varios/as

**sew** coser

**sex** sexo m

**shade** sombra f

**shake** agitar

**shallow** poco profundo

**shame** vergüenza f

**shampoo and set** lavar y marcar

**share** compartir

**sharp** afilado/a

**shave** afeitarse

**she** ella

**sheep** oveja f

**sheet** sábana f

**shelf** estante m

**shellfish** mariscos mpl

**sheltered** abrigado/a

**shine** brillo m

**shingle** tablilla f

**shingles** herpes m

**ship** barco m

**shirt** camisa f

**shock absorber** amortiguador m

**shoe** zapato m

**shoelace** cordón m

**shop** tienda f

**shop assistant** dependiente/a m/f

**shop window** vitrina f, vidriera f

**shopping centre** centro comercial

**shore** costa, orilla f

**short** corto/a

**short-cut** atajo m

**short-sighted** miope

**shorts** pantalones cortos

**should** deber

**shoulder** hombro m

**shout (n)** grito m

**shout (vb)** gritar

**show (n)** espectáculo m

**show (vb)** mostrar

**shower** ducha f

**shrimp** camarón m

**shrink** encoger

**shut** cerrar

**shutter** contraventana f

**shy** tímido/a

**sick, I'm going to be sick!** enfermo/a, ¡Voy a vomitar!
**side** lado m
**side dish** acompañamiento m
**sidewalk** acera f, vereda f
**sieve** colador m
**sight** vista f
**sightseeing** turismo m
**sign (n)** anuncio m
**sign (vb)** firmar
**signal** señal f
**signature** firma f
**signpost** poste indicador
**silence** silencio m
**silk** seda f
**silly** tonto/a
**silver** plata f
**similar** como, parecido/a
**simple** sencillo/a
**sing** cantar
**singer** cantante m/f
**single** solo, soltero/a
**single bed** cama de una plaza
**single room** habitación para uno/single
**single ticket** billete de ida
**sink** fregadero m
**sister** hermana f
**sister-in-law** cuñada f
**sit** sentarse
**size** tamaño, número m
**skate (n)** patín m

**skate (vb)** patinar
**skating rink** pista de patinaje
**ski (n)** esquí m
**ski (vb)** esquiar
**ski boot** bota para esquí
**ski jump** salto de esquí
**ski slope** pista para esquiar
**skin** piel f
**skirt** falda f
**sky** cielo m
**sledge** trineo m
**sleep** dormir
**sleeper, sleeping car** coche dormitorio
**sleeping bag** saco de dormir
**sleeping pill** pastilla para dormir, somnífero m
**sleepy** con sueño
**slice** rebanada f
**slide (n, photo)** diapositiva f
**slide (vb)** deslizarse
**slip** resbalarse
**slippers** zapatillas fpl
**slippery** resbaladizo/a
**Slovak** eslovaco
**Slovak Republic** República de Eslovaquia
**slow** lento/a
**slowly** despacio
**small** pequeño/a, chico/a
**smell** oler
**smile (vb)** sonreír
**smoke (n)** humo m

ENGLISH → SPANISH

**smoke (vb)** fumar
**smoked salmon** salmón ahumado
**snack** tentempie **m**, bocadillo **m**
**snake** serpiente **f**
**sneeze** estornudar
**snore** roncar
**snorkel** tubo de respiración
**snow, it is snowing** nieve, está nevando
**soaking solution** liquído para remojar
**soap** jabón **m**
**soap powder** jabón en polvo
**sober** sobrio/a
**socket (elec)** enchufe **m**
**socks** calcetines **mpl**, medias **fpl**
**soda** soda **f**
**soft** blando/a, suave
**soft drink** refesco **m**, bebida **f**
**sole (fish)** lenguado **m**
**sole (shoe)** suela **f**
**soluble** soluble
**some** unos/as, algunos/as
**someone, somebody** alguien, alguna persona
**something** algo
**sometimes** a veces
**somewhere** en algún lugar
**son** hijo **m**

**son-in-law** yerno **m**
**song** canción **f**
**soon** pronto
**sore** dolorido/a
**sore, it's sore** duele, tengo dolor
**sore throat** dolor de garganta
**Sorry!** ¡Lo siento! ¡Disculpa!
**sort** tipo **m**
**soup** sopa **f**
**sour** agrio/a
**south** sur **m**
**South Africa** Sudáfrica
**South African (adj, n)** sudafricano/a **m/f**
**souvenir** recuerdo **m**
**spade** pala **f**
**Spain** España
**Spaniard, Spanish** español/a **m/f**
**spanner** llave **f**, llave de tuercas
**spare part** parte de repuesto
**spare tyre** neumático de repuesto
**spark plug** bujía **f**
**sparkling** con gas
**speak** hablar
**speciality** especialidad **f**
**spectacles** lentes **m/f**, gafas **fpl**, anteojos **mpl**
**speed** velocidad **f**
**speed limit** límite de velocidad

**speedometer** velocímetro m

**spell** deletrear

**spend (money)** gastar

**spend (time)** pasar

**spice** especia f

**spider** araña f

**spill** derramar

**spin-dryer** secadora f

**spinach** espinacas fpl

**spine** espinazo m

**spirit (soul)** espíritu m

**spirits (drink)** licores mpl

**splinter** astilla f

**spoil** arruinar

**spoke (of wheel)** rayo m

**sponge** esponja f

**sponge cake** bizcocho m

**spoon** cuchara f

**sprain (n)** torcedura f

**sprain (vb)** torcer

**spring (season)** primavera f

**square** cuadro m, plaza f

**stadium** estadio m

**stain** mancha f

**stairs** escalera f

**stale** rancio/a

**stall** puesto m

**stamp** sello m, estampilla f

**staple (n, food)** alimento básico

**staple (vb)** grapar

**star** estrella f

**start** comenzar, empezar

**starter (car)** arranque

**station** estación f

**stationer's** papelería f

**stationery** artículos de escritorio

**statue** estatua f

**stay** quedarse, parar

**steal** robar

**steam** vapor m

**steep** empinado/a

**steer** dirigir

**steering wheel** volante m

**step** escalón m

**stepfather** padrastro m

**stepmother** madrastra f

**stew** guiso m

**stick (vb)** pegar

**sticking plaster** esparadrapo m

**still (yet)** todavía

**still (quiet)** quieto

**sting (n)** picadura f

**sting (vb)** picar

**stitch** puntada f

**stock (soup)** caldo m

**stocking** media f

**stolen** robado

**stomach** estómago m

**stomachache** dolor de estómago

**stone** piedra f

**stop** parar

**stop sign** pare

**stopover** parada f

**store (n)** tienda f

ENGLISH → SPANISH

ENGLISH → SPANISH

**store (vb)** almacenar
**storey** piso m, planta f
**storm** tormenta f
**straight** derecho/a
**straight on** siga derecho
**straightaway**
  directamente
**strange** raro/a
**strange, stranger**
  **(adj, n)** extraño/a m/f
**strap** correa f
**straw** paja f
**strawberry** fresa f,
  frutilla f
**stream** arroyo m
**street** calle f
**street map**
  mapa de calles
**strike (n)** huelga f
**string** cordel m
**striped** rayado/a
**stroke (n)** apoplegía f
**strong** fuerte
**stuck** pegado
**student** estudiante m/f
**student discount**
  descuento de estudiante
**stuffed** lleno/a, relleno/a
**stupid** estúpido/a
**subtitle** subtítulo m
**suburb** barrio m
**subway** metro m
**suddenly** de repente
**suede** gamuza f
**sugar** azúcar m/f
**sugar-free**
  no contiene azúcar
**suit** traje m

**suitcase** maleta f
**summer** verano m
**summit** cumbre f
**sun** sol m
**sunblock** crema
  para el sol
**sunburn** quemadura
  de sol
**Sunday** domingo m
**sunglasses** gafas
  de sol
**sunny** soleado/a
**sunrise** amanecer m
**sunroof** techo corredizo
**sunset** atardecer m
**sunshade** sombrilla f
**sunshine** luz del sol
**sunstroke** insolación f
**suntan** bronceado m
**suntan lotion** crema
  bronceadora
**supper** cena f
**supplement**
  suplemento m
**sure** seguro/a
**surfboard**
  tabla de surfear
**surgery (doctor's**
  **rooms)** consultorio m
**surgery (procedure)**
  cirujía f
**surname** apellido m
**surrounded** rodeado
**suspension** suspensión f
**swallow (vb)** tragar
**swear (an oath)** jurar
**swear (curse)** decir
  palabrotas

ENGLISH → SPANISH

**swear word** palabrota f
**sweat (n)** transpiración f
**sweat (vb)** sudar
**sweater** suéter m
**Sweden** Suecia
**Swedish, Swede (adj, n)** sueco/a m/f
**sweet (adj)** dulce
**swell** hincharse
**swelling** hinchazón f
**swim** nadar
**swimming costume** traje de baño/bañador
**swing** balanceo m
**Swiss (adj, n)** suizo/a m/f
**Swiss-German** suizo-alemán
**switch** interruptor m
**switch off** apagar
**switch on** encender
**Switzerland** Suiza
**swollen** hinchado/a
**synagogue** sinagoga f

**T**
**table** mesa f
**table wine** vino de mesa
**tablecloth** mantel m
**tablespoon** cucharón m
**tailor** sastre m
**take** tomar
**take-away food** comida para llevar
**talcum powder** talco m
**talk** hablar
**tall** alto/a
**tampon** tampón m

**tangerine** clementina f
**tank** tanque m
**tape** cinta f
**tape measure** cinta para medir
**tape recorder** grabadora f
**taste (n)** gusto m
**tax** impuesto m
**taxi** taxi m
**taxi driver** conductor/a de taxi, taxista m/f
**taxi rank** parada de taxis
**tea** té m
**tea bag** bolsa de té
**teach** enseñar
**teacher** maestro/a, profesor/a m/f
**team** equipo m
**teapot** tetera f
**tear (n)** desgarrón m
**tear (vb)** desgarrar
**teaspoon** cucharilla f
**teat (bottle)** tetina f
**teeth** dentadura f
**telephone** teléfono m
**telephone call** llamada telefónica
**telephone directory** directorio telefónico, guía telefónica
**television** televisión f
**tell** decir
**temperature** temperatura f
**temple** templo m
**temporary** temporario

ENGLISH → SPANISH

**tendon** tendón m
**tennis** tenis m
**tennis court** cancha de tenis, pista de tennis
**tennis racket** raqueta de tenis
**tent** carpa f
**tent peg** estaca f
**terminal** terminal m
**thank** agradecer
**that** ese/esa m/f
**the** el/la/los/las
**theatre** teatro m
**theft** robo m
**there** allí/allá
**thermometer** termómetro m
**they** ellos/ellas
**thick** grueso/a
**thief** ladrón/ladrona m/f
**thigh** muslo m
**thin** flaco/a, delgado/a
**thing** cosa f
**think** pensar
**third-party insurance** seguro contra terceros
**thirsty** tener sed
**this** este/esta
**this morning** esta mañana
**this way** por aquí
**this week** esta semana
**thorn** espina f
**those** esos/esas
**thousand** mil m
**thread** hilado m
**throat** garganta f

**throat lozenges** pastillas/caramelos para la garganta
**through** a través de, por
**throw** echar
**thumb** pulgar m
**thunder** trueno m
**thunderstorm** tormenta f
**Thursday** jueves m
**ticket** billete m, boleto m
**ticket collector** revisor/a m/f
**ticket office** despacho de billetes
**tide, low tide, high tide** marea f, marea baja, marea alta
**tie** corbata f
**tight** apretado/a, tirante
**tights** medias fpl
**till (cash register)** caja f
**till (until)** hasta
**time** hora f
**timetable** horario m
**tin** lata f
**tin opener** abridor de latas
**tinfoil** papel metálico
**tiny** minúsculo/a
**tip** propina f
**tired** cansado/a
**tissue** tisú m
**to** a
**toad** sapo m
**today** hoy m

toe dedo del pie
together juntos/as
toilet baño m, servicios mpl
tolerate aguantar
toll, toll road peaje m, camino de peaje
tomato tomate m
tomato juice jugo de tomate
tomorrow mañana m
tomorrow morning/ afternoon/evening mañana por la mañana/ tarde/noche
tongue lengua f
tonight esta noche
tonsillitis amigdalitis f
too también
too much demasiado
tool herramienta f
toolkit caja de herramientas
tooth diente m
toothache dolor de muelas
toothbrush cepillo de dientes
toothpick escarbadientes
top parte de arriba
top floor el piso más alto
topless sin camiseta
torch linterna f
torn rasgado
total total m
tough duro/a, fuerte
tour viaje m

tour guide guía de turismo
tour operator operador de turismo
tow remolcar
towel toalla f
tower torre f
town ciudad f
town hall sala municipal, ayuntamiento m
toy juguete m
tracksuit chándal m
traffic tráfico m
traffic jam atascamiento m, embotellamiento m
traffic light semáforo m
trailer remolque m
train tren m
tram tranvía m
tranquillizer droga tranquilizante
translate traducir
translation traducción f
translator traductor/a m/f
trash basura f
travel viajar
travel agent agente de viajes
travel documents documentos de viajes
travel sickness mareo m
traveller's cheque cheque de viaje
tray bandeja f

ENGLISH → SPANISH

**tree** árbol m
**trolley** carro m
**trouble** problemas mpl
**trousers** pantalones mpl
**trout** trucha f
**truck** camión m
**true** verdadero/a
**trunk (of car)** baúl,
  maletero m
**try** intentar
**try on** probarse
**tube** tubo m
**tuna** atún m
**tunnel** subterráneo m,
  túnel m
**turkey** pavo m
**Turkey** Turquía
**Turkish, Turk (adj, n)**
  turco/a m/f
**turn** volver
**turn around** darse vuelta
**turn off** apagar
**turquoise** turquesa f
**tweezers** pinzas fpl
**twice** dos veces
**twin beds** camas
  gemelas
**twins** gemelos
**type** tipo m
**typical** típico/a
**tyre** neumático m
**tyre pressure** presión
  en los neumáticos

**U**
**ugly** feo/a
**ulcer** úlcera f
**umbrella** paraguas m

**uncle** tío m
**uncomfortable**
  incómodo/a
**unconscious**
  inconciente
**under** bajo
**underdone** poco hecho
**underground (adj)**
  subterráneo/a
**underground
  (n, subway)** metro m
**underpants** ropa interior
**understand**
  comprender, entender
**underwear** ropa interior
**unemployed**
  desempleado/a
**United Kingdom** Reino
  Unido
**United States**
  Estados Unidos
**university** universidad f
**unleaded petrol**
  combustible sin plomo
**unlimited** ilimitado/a
**unlock** abrir
**unpack** desembalar
**unscrew** destornillar
**until** hasta
**unusual** insólito/a
**up** arriba
**up-market** superior
**upside down** al revés
**upstairs** al piso de arriba
**urgent** urgente
**us** nos, nosotros/as
**use** usar
**useful** útil

**usual** corriente
**usually** generalmente

# V

**vacancy** habitación libre
**vacation** vacaciones fpl
**vaccine** vacuna f
**vacuum cleaner**
  aspiradora f
**valid** válido/a
**valley** valle m
**valuable** de valor
**value** valor m
**valve** válvula f
**van** camioneta f
**VAT** Impuesto sobre
  Valor Añadido (IVA)
**veal** ternera f
**vegetables**
  verduras fpl,
  vegetales mpl
**vegetarian**
  vegetariano/a m/f
**vehicle** vehículo m
**vein** vena f
**vending machine**
  máquina expendedora
**venereal disease**
  enfermedad de
  trasmisión sexual
**very** muy
**vest** camisetilla f
**vet (veterinarian)**
  veterinario/a m/f
**via** vía, por
**Vienna** Viena
**view** vista f
**village** pueblo m

**vinegar** vinagre m
**vineyard** viñedo m
**violet (adj, n)** violeta f
**virus** virus m
**visa** visa f
**visit** visitar
**visiting hours**
  horario de visita
**visitor** visitante m/f
**voice** voz f
**volcano** volcán m
**voltage** voltaje m
**vomit** vomitar
**voucher** vale m,
  cupón m

# W

**wage** salario, sueldo m
**waist** cintura f
**waistcoat** chaleco m
**wait** esperar
**waiter/waitress**
  camarero/a, mozo/a m/f
**waiting room**
  sala de espera
**wake up** despertar
**wake-up call**
  llamada para despertar
**Wales** Gales
**walk** caminar, andar
**wall** muro m, pared f
**wallet** billetera f
**walnut** nuez f
**want** querer
**war** guerra f
**ward (hospital)** sala f
**wardrobe**
  guardarropa m

ENGLISH → SPANISH

137

ENGLISH → SPANISH

**warehouse** almacén m
**warm** cálido/a
**wash** lavar
**washbasin** lavabo m
**washing powder** polvo de lavar
**washing-up liquid** líquido para lavar, detergente m
**wasp** avispa f
**waste** residuo m
**waste bin** bote de residuos/bote de basura
**watch (n)** reloj m
**watch (vb)** mirar
**watch strap** correa de reloj
**water** agua f
**watermelon** sandía f
**waterproof** a prueba de agua
**water-skiing** esquí acuático
**wave** ola f
**we** nosotros/as
**weak** débil
**wear** llevar, usar
**weather** tiempo m
**weather forecast** pronóstico del tiempo
**web** red f
**wedding** boda f
**wedding present** regalo de boda
**wedding ring** anillo de boda
**Wednesday** miércoles m

**week – last week, this week, next week, a week ago** semana f – semana pasada, esta semana, semana próxima, hace una semana
**weekday** día de semana
**weekend** fin de semana
**weekly** semanalmente
**weigh** pesar
**weight** peso m
**weird** raro/a
**welcome** bienvenido/a
**well** bien
**Welsh, Welshman, Welshwoman (adj, n)** galés/galesa m/f
**were** era/estaba
**west** oeste m
**wet** mojado/a
**wetsuit** traje de agua
**What?** ¿Qué?
**What is wrong?** ¿Hay algo mal/malo?
**What's the matter?** ¿Qué pasa?
**What's the time?** ¿Qué hora es?
**wheel** rueda f
**wheel clamp** cepo m
**wheelchair** silla de rueda
**When?** ¿Cuándo?
**Where?** ¿Dónde?
**Which?** ¿Cuál?
**while** mientras

**whipped cream** nata montada

**white** blanco/a

**Who?** ¿Quién?

**whole (adj)** entero/a

**whole (n)** todo m

**wholemeal bread** pan integral de trigo

**Whose?** ¿De quién?

**Why?** ¿Por qué?

**wide** ancho/a

**widower, widow** viudo/a m/f

**wife** esposa f

**wig** peluca f

**win** ganar

**wind** viento m

**window** ventana f

**window seat** asiento en ventanilla

**windscreen** parabrisas m

**windscreen wiper** limpiaparabrisas m

**windy** ventoso/a

**wine** vino m

**wine glass** copa f

**winter** invierno m

**wire** cable m

**wish** desear

**with** con

**without** sin

**witness** testigo m/f

**wolf** lobo m

**woman** mujer f

**wood** madera f

**wool** lana f

**word** palabra f

**work** trabajar

**world** mundo m

**worried** preocupado/a

**worse** peor

**worth** de valor

**wrap up** envolver

**wrapping paper** papel de envolver

**wrinkles** arrugas fpl

**wrist** muñeca f

**write** escribir

**writing paper** papel de escribir

**X**

**X-ray** radiografía f

**Y**

**yacht** yate m

**year** año m

**yellow** amarillo/a

**yellow pages** páginas amarillas

**yes** sí

**yesterday** ayer m

**yolk** yema f

**you** tú

**young** jóven

**your** tu

**youth hostel** albergue juvenil

**Z**

**zero** cero m

**zipper, zip fastener** cremallera f

**zone** zona f

**zoo** jardín zoológico

ENGLISH → SPANISH

**SPANISH → ENGLISH**

## A

**a** to
**a él** to him
**a la parrilla** grilled
**a pesar de** although
**a prueba de agua** waterproof
**a puertas adentro** indoors
**a través de** through
**a veces** sometimes
**abadía f** abbey
**abajo** downstairs
**abeja f** bee
**abierto/a** open
**abogado/a m/f** lawyer
**abono m** season ticket
**aborto m** abortion
**abridor de botellas** bottle opener
**abridor de latas** can opener, tin opener
**abrigado/a** sheltered
**abrigo m** coat, jacket, overcoat
**abrigo de piel** fur coat
**abrir** unlock
**abrochar** fasten
**absceso m** abscess
**abuelo/a m/f** grandfather, grandmother
**abuelos mpl** grandparents
**aburrido** boring
**acá** here, over here
**acampar** camp (vb)
**acantilado m** cliff
**accidente m** accident

**accidente de tráfico** road accident
**acedía f** heartburn
**aceite m** oil
**aceite de oliva** olive oil
**aceituna f** olive
**acelerador m** accelerator
**acento m** accent
**aceptar** accept
**acera f** sidewalk
**acompañamiento m** side dish
**aconsejar** advise
**acostarse** lie down
**acuerdo m** agreement
**adaptador m** adapter
**adelantar** overtake
**adentro** inside
**adiós** goodbye
**aduana f** customs
**adulto/a m/f** adult (adj, n)
**aeropuerto m** airport
**afeitarse** shave
**afilado/a** sharp
**afuera** out, outside
**afueras** countryside, outskirts
**agarrar** catch
**agenda f** diary
**agente de policía** policeman/woman
**agente de viajes** travel agent
**agente inmobilario/a** estate agent
**agitar** shake

**agotado/a** exhausted
**agradable** nice
**agradecer** thank
**agradecido/a** grateful
**agrio/a** sour
**agua** f water
**agua mineral** mineral water
**agua potable** drinking water
**aguamala** f jellyfish
**aguantar** put up with, tolerate
**águila** f eagle
**aguja** f needle
**aguja de tejer** knitting needle
**aguja hipodérmica** hypodermic needle
**agujero** m hole, leak
**ahora** now
**ahorrar** save
**aire** m air
**aire acondicionado** air conditioning
**aislado/a** secluded
**ajedrez** m chess
**ajo** m garlic
**ajustar** fasten
**ajustar el cinturón de seguridad** fasten seatbelt
**al aire libre** outdoors
**al fondo** at the bottom
**al piso de arriba** upstairs
**al principio** at first
**al revés** upside down

**aladeltismo** hang-gliding
**alambrada** f fence
**alba** f dawn (n)
**albergue** m hostel
**albergue juvenil** youth hostel
**alegría** f joy
**alemán, alemana** m/f German (adj, n)
**Alemania** Germany
**aletas** fpl flippers
**alfiler** m pin
**alfombra** f carpet, rug
**alga** f seaweed
**algo** something
**algodón** m cotton
**algodón hidrófilo** cotton wool
**alguien** someone, somebody
**alguna persona** someone, somebody
**algunos/as** some
**alicates** mpl pliers
**alimentar** feed (vb)
**alimento** m food
**alimento básico** staple (food)
**aliño** m salad dressing
**allá** over there
**allí/allá** there
**almacén** m food shop, warehouse
**almacenar** store (vb)
**almendra** f almond
**almohada** f pillow
**almohadón** m cushion

SPANISH → ENGLISH

**almuerzo m** lunch

**alojamiento m** accommodation

**alojamiento con cocina** self-catering

**alquilar** let, hire, rent (vb)

**alquiler m** rent (n)

**alquiler de coches** car hire

**alto/a** high, tall

**altura f** height

**amable** kind

**amanecer m** sunrise, dawn

**amapola f** poppy

**amar** love (vb)

**amarillo/a** yellow

**amarradero m** mooring

**ámbar m** amber

**ambos** both

**ambulancia f** ambulance

**amigable** friendly

**amigdalitis f** tonsillitis

**amigo/a m/f** friend

**amigo/a invisible** penfriend

**amigo/a por carta** penfriend

**amor m** love (n)

**amortiguador m** shock absorber

**ampliación f** enlargement

**ampolla f** blister

**amueblado** furnished

**analgésico m** painkiller

**ananá m** pineapple

**ancho/a** wide

**andar** go, walk

**andar conducir** drive, go by car

**andar en bicicleta** cycle (vb)

**andar manejar** drive, go by car

**andén m** platform

**anestésico m** anaesthetic

**angosto/a** narrow

**anguila f** eel

**anillo m** ring (n)

**anillo de boda** wedding ring

**animal m** animal

**animal doméstico** pet

**aniversario m** anniversary

**anoche** last night

**año m** year

**Año Nuevo** New Year

**anteojos mpl** spectacles, glasses

**antes** before

**antiácido** antacid

**anticonceptivo m/f** contraceptive

**antiparras fpl** goggles

**anual** annual

**anuncio m** sign (n)

**apagado/a** dull, gloomy

**apagar** switch off, turn off

**aparcar** park (vb)

**apartamento** m apartment, flat
**apellido** m surname
**apenas** hardly
**apendicitis** f appendicitis
**apio** m celery
**aplazar** postpone
**apoplegía** f stroke (n)
**apostar** bet
**aprender** learn
**apretado/a** tight
**aproximadamente** about, approximately, roughly
**aquí** here, over here
**araña** f spider
**arañazo** m scratch (n)
**árbol** m tree
**arbusto** m bush
**archivo** m file (folder)
**área** f area
**arena** f sand
**arma** f gun
**armada** f navy
**armario** m cupboard, locker
**aros** mpl earrings
**arranque** starter (car)
**arreglar** arrange, fix
**arrendar** lease (vb)
**arrestar** arrest
**arriba** up
**arroyo** m stream
**arroz** m rice
**arrugas** fpl wrinkles
**arruinar** spoil
**arte** m art

**artesanía** f craft
**artículos de escritorio** stationery
**artista** m/f artist
**ascensor** m lift, elevator
**asiento** m seat
**asiento de coche para niños** child car seat
**asiento en el pasillo** aisle seat
**asiento en ventanilla** window seat
**asociarse** join
**áspero/a** rough
**aspiradora** f vacuum cleaner
**asqueroso/a** revolting
**astilla** f splinter
**asunto** m matter
**asunto escrito** printed matter
**atacar** attack (vb)
**atajo** m short-cut
**ataque** m attack (n)
**ataque al corazón** heart attack
**atardecer** m sunset
**atascamiento** m traffic jam
**ático** m attic
**atropellar** knock over
**atún** m tuna
**audiencia** f audience
**audífono** m hearing aid
**auricular** m receiver (telephone)

SPANISH → ENGLISH

**auriculares** mpl
earphones, headphones
**auténtico/a** genuine
**auto** m car
**autobús** m bus
**autocar** m coach
**autopista** f freeway,
motorway
**autoservicio** m
self-service
**avalancha** f avalanche
**ave** f bird
**avellana** f hazelnut
**avena** f oats
**avenida** f avenue
**avería** f breakdown
(car)
**avión** m aeroplane,
plane
**aviso** m advertisement
**avispa** f wasp
**ayer** m yesterday
**¡Ayuda!** Help!
**ayudar** help (vb)
**ayuntamiento** m
town hall
**azúcar** m/f sugar
**azul** blue
**azul marino** navy blue

**B**
**bacalao** m cod
**bache** m pothole
**bahía** f bay
**bailar** dance (vb)
**bajar** get off
**bajas calorías** low fat
**bajo** below, under

**bajo/a** low
**bajo llave** locked in
**balanceo** m swing
**balanza** f scales
**balcón** m balcony
**balde** m bucket
**bandeja** f tray
**bañera** f bath
**baño** m bathroom,
cloakroom, lavatory,
toilet
**baño de hombres**
gents' toilet
**baño de mujeres**
ladies' toilet
**bar gay** gay bar
**barato/a** cheap
**barba** f beard
**barbería** f barber's
shop
**barbilla** f chin
**barco** m boat, ship
**barra** f loaf
**barra de chocolate**
bar of chocolate
**barranca abajo**
downhill
**barril** m barrel
**barrio** m area, district,
suburb
**barro** m mud
**bastante** fairly
**basura** f litter, refuse,
rubbish, trash
**bata** f dressing gown
**batería descargada**
flat battery
**baúl** m trunk

**beber** drink (vb)
**bebida f** drink, soft drink
**belga m/f** Belgian (adj, n)
**Bélgica** Belgium
**besar** kiss (vb)
**beso m** kiss (n)
**biblioteca f** library
**bicicleta f** bicycle
**bien** OK, well
**bienvenido/a** welcome
**bigote m** moustache
**billete m** ticket
**billete abierto** open ticket
**billete aéreo** air ticket
**billete de ida** single ticket
**billete de ida y vuelta** return ticket
**billete de temporada** season ticket
**billetera f** wallet
**binoculares** binoculars
**bizcocho m** sponge cake
**blanco/a** white
**blando/a** soft
**blanquear** bleach (vb)
**bloqueado** blocked
**bloqueo automático** central locking
**blusa f** blouse
**boca f** mouth
**bocadillo m** sandwich, snack
**bocina f** horn (car)
**boda f** wedding
**bodega f** cellar

**boleto m** ticket
**boleto de estaciona-miento** parking ticket
**boli m** pen
**bolígrafo m** ballpoint pen
**bolsa f** bag, carrier bag
**bolsa de agua caliente** hot-water bottle
**bolsa de plástico** plastic bag
**bolsillo m** pocket
**bolsita de té** tea bag
**bolso m** handbag, purse
**bomberos mpl** fire brigade
**bombilla f** light bulb
**bombones mpl** chocolates
**bonito/a** beautiful, pretty
**borde m** border, edge
**borracho/a m/f** drunk (adj, n)
**bosque m** forest
**bota para esquí** ski boot
**botas fpl** boots
**bote m** boat, dinghy
**bote de residuos/basura** waste bin
**botella f** bottle
**botón m** button
**bragas fpl** knickers, panties
**brandy m** brandy
**brillante** bright

**brillo** m shine
**brisa** f breeze
**broche** m brooch
**broches para la ropa**
  clothes peg
**broma** f joke
**bronceado** m suntan
**bronquitis** f bronchitis
**Bruselas** Brussels
**bucear** dive
**buena suerte**
  good luck
**buenas noches**
  good night
**buenas tardes**
  good afternoon,
  good evening
**bueno/a** good
**buenos días** good
  morning, good day
**bufanda** f scarf
**bujía** f spark plug
**bulbo** m bulb (plant)
**buscar** fetch, look for
**buzón** m letterbox,
  postbox

**C**
**caballo** m horse
**cabello** m hair
**cabeza** f head
**cabina** f cabin
**cabina telefónica**
  phone booth
**cable** m wire
**cable de extensión**
  extension lead

**cables de conexion
  de batería**
  jump leads
**cabra** f goat
**cacahuete** m peanut
**cacao** m cocoa
**cacerola** f pan
**cada** each, every
**cada hora** hourly (adj)
**cada uno** everyone
**cadera** f hip
**caducar** expire
**caer** fall
**café** m coffee
**café helado** m
  iced coffee
**café instantáneo**
  instant coffee
**caja** f box, carton, cash
  desk, cash register, till
**caja de cambios**
  gearbox
**caja de fusibles**
  fuse box
**caja de herramientas**
  toolkit
**caja fuerte** safe (n)
**cajero/a** m/f cashier
**cajero automático**
  auto-teller,
  cash dispenser
**cajón** m drawer
**calambre** m cramp
**calcetines** mpl socks
**calculadora** f calculator
**caldo** m stock
**calefacción** f heating

**calefacción central** central heating
**calefactor** m heater
**calidad** f quality
**cálido/a** warm
**caliente** hot
**calle** f road, street
**calle de una sola mano** one-way street
**calle principal/mayor** main road
**calma** calm
**calor** m heat
**calzada** f pavement
**cama** f bed
**cama de una plaza** single bed
**cama doble** double bed
**cámara de aire** inner tube
**camarera** f chambermaid
**camarero/a** m/f waiter, waitress
**camarón** m shrimp
**camas gemelas** twin beds
**cambiador** m fitting room
**cambiar** change (vb)
**cambio** m change, exchange (n)
**caminar** walk
**camino** m road
**camino circular** ring road

**camino de peaje** toll road
**camión** m truck
**camión de reparación de averías** breakdown van
**camioneta** f lorry, van
**camisa** f shirt
**camisetilla** f vest
**campamento** m campsite
**campamento de remolques** caravan site
**campana** f bell
**campo** m countryside, field
**campo de golf** golf course
**Canadá** Canada
**canal** m canal, channel
**Canal de la Mancha** English Channel
**canasta** f basket
**cancelación** f cancellation
**cancelar** cancel
**cáncer** m cancer
**cancha de tenis** tennis court
**canción** f song
**candado** m padlock
**cangrejo** m crab
**canoa** f canoe
**cansado/a** tired
**cantante** m/f singer
**cantar** sing

SPANISH → ENGLISH

**cantidad f** amount, quantity
**caña de pescar** fishing rod
**cañería f** pipe (plumbing)
**capilla f** chapel
**capital f** capital (city)
**capital m** capital (money)
**capó/capota m/f** bonnet, hood (car)
**capucha f** hood (garment)
**cara f** face
**caramelos para la garganta** throat lozenges
**carbón m** charcoal, coal
**carburador m** carburettor
**cárcel f** prison
**cargar** carry, charge
**carnada f** bait
**carne f** meat
**carne de puerco/ cerdo** pork
**carne de vaca f** beef
**carne medio hecha** medium rare (meat)
**carne picada** minced meat
**carné m** card
**carné de identidad** identity card
**carnet de conducir** driving licence

**carnicero/a m/f** butcher
**caro/a** expensive
**carpa f** tent
**carpeta f** file (folder)
**carpintero/a m/f** carpenter
**carrera f** race (sport)
**carrera de caballos** horse racing
**carretera f** road
**carretera de circunvalación** bypass (road)
**carretera en obras** road works
**carril m** lane
**carrito para equipaje** luggage trolley
**carro m** car, trolley
**carta f** card, letter
**carta de vinos** wine list
**cartera f** handbag
**carterista f** pickpocket
**cartero/a m/f** postman/postwoman
**cartón m** cardboard
**casa f** home, house
**casado/a** married
**casco m** helmet, crash helmet
**casi** almost, nearly
**casilla de correo** post office box
**caso m** case
**cassette f** cassette
**castaño m** chestnut
**castillo m** castle

**catedral** f cathedral
**católico/a** m/f
  Catholic (adj, n)
**caucho** m rubber
**cazar** hunt
**cebo** m bait
**cebolla** f onion
**cebolleta** f chives
**celoso/a** jealous
**cementerio** m
  cemetery
**cena** f dinner, supper
**centígrado** Centigrade
**centímetro** m
  centimetre
**centro** m centre
**centro comercial**
  shopping centre
**centro de la ciudad**
  city centre
**centro musical**
  CD player
**cepillo** m brush (n)
**cepillo de dientes**
  toothbrush
**cepillo de pelo**
  hairbrush
**cepillo de uñas**
  nailbrush
**cepillo para fregar**
  scrubbing brush
**cepo** m wheel clamp
**cera** f polish (n)
**cerámica** f pottery
**cerca** near, nearby (adv)
**cercano/a** near,
  nearby (adj)
**cerdo** m pig

**cereza** f cherry
**cero** m zero
**cerrado/a** closed,
  blocked
**cerradura** f lock (n)
**cerrar** lock, lock out,
  shut
**certeza** certain
**certificado** m
  certificate
**certificado de
  nacimiento**
  birth certificate
**certificar** register (vb)
**cerveza** f beer
**cerveza de barril/
  tirada** draught beer
**cerveza rubia** lager
**césped** m grass
**cesta** f basket
**chaleco** m waistcoat,
  pullover
**chaleco salvavidas**
  life jacket
**champán** m
  champagne
**champiñon** m
  mushroom
**chancletas** fpl
  flip-flops
**chándal** m tracksuit
**chaqueta** f jacket
**chaval/a** m/f child
**cheque** m cheque
**cheque de viaje**
  traveller's cheque
**chícharo** m pea
**chicle** m chewing gum

**chico/a** small
**chico/a** m/f child
**chimenea** f chimney
**China** China
**chocar** crash (vb)
**chocolate** m chocolate
**chófer** m driver
**chupete** m dummy,
  pacifier
**chupón** lollipop
**ciego/a** blind (adj)
**cielo** m sky
**cielo raso** ceiling
**ciertamente** certainly
**cigarrillo** m cigarette
**cine** m cinema
**cinta** f ribbon, tape
**cinta adhesiva** f
  adhesive tape
**cinta para medir**
  tape measure
**cintura** f waist
**cinturón** m belt
**cinturón de seguridad**
  safety belt, seatbelt
**cinturón salvavidas**
  life belt
**círculo** m circle
**ciruela** f plum
**cirujía** f surgery
  (procedure)
**cisterna** f cistern
**cistitis** f cystitis
**cita** f appointment, date
**ciudad** f city, town
**ciudadano/a** m/f
  citizen

**claro** absolutely,
  certainly
**claro/a** clear, light
  (adj, colour)
**clase** f class, lesson
**clase económica**
  economy class
**clavícula** f collarbone
**clavija** f peg
**clementina** f tangerine
**cliente** m/f client,
  customer
**clima** m climate
**clínica** f clinic
**club de golf** golf club
  (place)
**cobertor** quilt,
  bedspread
**cobrar excesiva-
  mente** overcharge
**Coca Cola** f Coke
**coche** m car
**coche comedor**
  buffet car
**coche de alquiler**
  hire car
**coche dormitorio**
  sleeper, sleeping car
**cochecito** m pram
**cochecito de niño**
  buggy
**cocina** f cooker, kitchen
**cocinar** cook (vb)
**cocinero/a** m/f
  cook (n), chef
**cocinilla** f kitchenette
**coco** m coconut
**código** m code

**código postal** postal code
**codo** m elbow
**coger** catch
**cola** f queue (n)
**colador** m colander, sieve
**colchón** f mattress
**colega** m/f colleague
**colgar** hang up (telephone)
**coliflor** f cauliflower
**collar** m necklace
**color** m colour
**colorear** dye (vb)
**colorete** m blusher
**combustible** m gas, fuel, petrol
**combustible sin plomo** unleaded petrol
**comedia** f comedy
**comedor** m dining room
**comenzar** start
**comer** eat
**comida** f food, meal
**comida de campo** picnic
**comida envenenada** food poisoning
**comida para bebé** baby food
**comida para llevar** take-away food
**comisaría** f police station
**como** like, similar to

**¿Cómo?** How?
**¿Cómo estás?** How do you do? How are you?
**cómoda** f chest of drawers
**cómodo/a** comfortable
**compañero/a** m/f partner (companion)
**compañía** f company
**compartimento** m compartment
**compartir** share
**compás** m compass
**complejo turístico** resort
**completamente** completely, quite
**compositor/a** m/f composer
**comprar** buy
**comprender** understand
**compresa higiénica** sanitary pads
**comprometido/a** engaged (to be married)
**computadora** f computer
**Comunidad Europea** EC
**con** with
**con experiencia** experienced
**con fluidez** fluent
**con frecuencia** often
**con gas** fizzy, sparkling
**con hambre** hungry

151

**SPANISH → ENGLISH**

**con sueño** sleepy
**concesión f** concession
**conciente** conscious
**concierto m** concert
**condición f** condition
**condimento m** seasoning
**condimento para ensalada** salad dressing
**condón m** condom
**conducción a la derecha** right-hand drive
**conducción a la izquierda** left-hand drive
**conducir** drive
**conductor/a m/f** driver
**conductor/a de taxi** taxi driver
**conejo/a m/f** rabbit
**conexión f** connection (elec)
**conferencia f** conference
**confirmación f** confirmation
**confirmar** confirm
**confundido/a** confused
**confundir** mix up (vb)
**confusión f** mix-up (n)
**congelado/a** frozen
**congelador m** freezer
**conmoción cerebral** concussion
**conocer** know

**consejo m** advice
**construir** build
**consulado m** consulate
**consultorio m** surgery (doctor's rooms)
**contacto m** contact (n)
**contador m** meter
**contaminado** polluted
**contenedor de gasolina** petrol can
**contestar** reply (vb)
**continuar** continue
**contra** against
**contrato m** contract
**contrato de alquiler** lease (n)
**contraventana f** shutter
**control de pasaporte** pass control
**contundente** blunt
**conveniente** convenient
**copa f** wine glass
**copiar** copy
**corazón m** heart
**corbata f** tie
**corcho m** cork
**cordel m** string
**cordero m** lamb, mutton
**cordón m** shoelace
**coro m** choir
**corona f** crown
**correa f** strap
**correa de reloj** watch strap

**correa del ventilador**
fanbelt
**correctamente**
properly
**correcto/a** correct (adj)
**correo** m mail, post (n)
**correo aéreo** airmail
**correo central** main
post office
**correo certificado**
registered mail
**correr** run, jog (vb)
**corriente** usual
**corriente** f current (n),
draught
**cortar** chop, cut
**corte de electricidad**
power cut
**corte de pelo** haircut
**cortijo** m farmhouse
**cortina** f curtain
**corto/a** short
**cosa** f thing
**cosecha** f harvest
**coser** sew
**costa** f coast, seaside
**coste, costo** m cost
**costilla** f rib
**costumbre** f custom
**creer** believe
**crema** f cream
**crema bronceadora**
suntan lotion
**crema hidratante**
moisturizer
**crema limpiadora**
cleansing lotion

**crema para el sol**
sunblock
**crema pastelera**
custard
**cremallera** f zipper,
zip fastener
**crepe** f pancake
**criada** f maid
**cristal** m crystal
**cruce** m crossing,
junction, intersection
**cruce a nivel** level
crossing
**cruce de caminos**
crossroads
**crucero** m cruise (n)
**crucigrama** m
crossword puzzle
**crudo/a** raw
**cruz** m cross (n)
**cruzar** cross (vb)
**cuaderno** m notebook
**cuadro** m painting,
square
**¿Cuál?** Which?
**cualquier cosa**
anything
**cualquiera** anybody
**¿Cuándo?** When?
**¿Cuánto/a?** How
many?
**¿Cuánto es?** How
much is it?
**cuarentena** f
quarantine
**cuarto** m quarter, room
**cuatro por cuatro**
four-wheel drive

SPANISH → ENGLISH

**cubertería f** cutlery
**cubo m** bucket, pail
**cubo de la basura**
  bin, dustbin
**cucaracha f** cockroach
**cuchara f** spoon
**cucharilla f** teaspoon
**cucharón m**
  tablespoon
**cuchillo m** knife
**cuello m** collar, neck
**cuenco m** bowl
**cuenta f** account, bill
**cuerda f** rope
**cuerno m** horn (animal)
**cuero m** leather
**cuerpo m** body
**cuesta abajo** downhill
**cuestión f** question
**cueva f** cave
**cuidado** careful
**cuidar** look after
**culpa f** fault
**cumbre f** summit
**cumpleaños m**
  birthday
**cuna f** cot
**cuna portable**
  carry-cot
**cuñada f** sister-in-law
**cuñado m**
  brother-in-law
**cupón m** voucher
**cura m** priest
**curso m** course
**curso de idioma**
  language course

# D

**dados mpl** dice
**daltónico/a**
  colour-blind
**dama f** lady
**daño m** damage
**dar** give
**dar marcha atrás**
  reverse (vb)
**darse cuenta** realize
**darse prisa** rush,
  hurry (vb)
**darse vuelta** roll, turn
  around
**dátil m** date (fruit)
**datos mpl** details
**de** from (origin), of
**de moda** fashionable
**de otra forma**
  otherwise (differently)
**¿De quién?** Whose?
**de repente** suddenly
**de valor** valuable,
  worth
**de vez en cuando**
  occasionally
**deber** must, have to,
  owe, should
**débil** weak
**decepcionado/a**
  disappointed
**decidir** decide
**decir** say, tell
**decir palabrotas**
  swear (curse)
**decisión f** decision
**dedo m** finger
**dedo del pie** toe

**defecto** m fault
**defectuoso/a** faulty
**definitivamente**
definitely
**dejar** leave, let, allow
**dejar encerrado**
lock out
**delantal** m apron
**deletrear** spell
**delgado/a** thin
**deliberadamente**
deliberately
**delicioso/a** delicious
**delito** m crime
**demasiado** plenty,
too much
**demora** f delay (n)
**dentadura** f teeth
**dentaduras** dentures
**dentista** m/f dentist
**dentro** among, inside
**dependiente/a** m/f
shop assistant
**depósito** m deposit
**derecho/a** right,
straight
**derramar** spill
**derretir** melt
**derribar** knock down
**derrumbarse**
collapse (vb)
**desagüe** m drain (n)
**desaparecer**
disappear
**desaparecido/a**
missing
**desarrollar** develop
**desastre** m disaster

**desayuno** m breakfast
**descafeinado/a**
decaffeinated
**descansar** rest (relax)
**desconectado**
disconnected
**descontar** deduct
**describir** describe
**descripción** f
description
**descubrir** discover
**descuento** m discount
**descuento de
estudiante**
student discount
**desde** from (time)
**desear** wish
**desembalar** unpack
**desempleado/a**
unemployed
**desfiladero** m pass (n)
**desgarrar** tear (vb)
**desgarrón** m tear (n)
**desierto** m desert
**desinfectante** m
disinfectant
**desinfectante bucal**
mouthwash
**deslizarse** slide (vb)
**desmaquillador para
ojos** eye make-up
remover
**desmayarse** faint (vb)
**despacho de billetes**
ticket office
**despacio** slowly
**desperfecto** m flaw

SPANISH → ENGLISH

**despertar** awake, wake up

**desprendimiento de tierras** landslide

**después** after, afterwards

**destino** m destination

**destornillador** m screwdriver

**destornillar** unscrew

**desviación** bypass

**desvío** m detour

**detalles** mpl details

**detergente** m cleaning solution, detergent, washing-up liquid

**detrás** behind

**deudas** fpl debts

**devolver** give back, refund (vb)

**día** m day

**día de semana** weekday

**día feriado** public holiday

**diabético/a** m/f diabetic (adj, n)

**diamante** m diamond

**diapositiva** f slide (photo)

**diariamente** daily

**diario** m diary

**diarrea** f diarrhoea

**dibujo** m drawing

**diccionario** m dictionary

**diciembre** m December

**diente** m tooth

**diesel** m diesel

**dieta** f diet

**diferencia** f difference

**diferente** different

**difícil** difficult

**Dinamarca** Denmark

**dínamo** f dynamo

**dinero** m money

**dinero efectivo** cash

**Dios** m God

**dirección** f direction

**directamente** straightaway

**directo/a** direct (adj)

**directorio telefónico** telephone directory

**dirigir** steer

**disco** m disk, record (n, music)

**disco de aparcamiento** parking disc

**disco duro** hard disk

**¿Disculpa?** Pardon?

**¡Disculpa!** Sorry!

**disculpa** f apology, excuse (n)

**discutir** quarrel (vb)

**disfrutar** enjoy

**disponible** available

**distancia** f distance

**distrito** m district

**diversión** f fun (n)

**divertido/a** fun (adj)

**divorciado** divorced

**dobladillo** m hem

**doblar** bend
**doble** double
**docena f** dozen
**documento m**
document, record
(legal)
**documento de**
**identidad** identity
card
**documentos de viajes**
travel documents
**doler** hurt (vb)
**dolor m** ache, pain
**dolor de cabeza**
headache
**dolor de espalda**
backache
**dolor de estómago**
stomachache
**dolor de garganta**
sore throat
**dolor de muelas**
toothache
**dolor de oídos**
earache
**dolorido/a** sore
**doloroso/a** painful
**doméstico/a** domestic
**domingo m** Sunday
**¿Dónde?** Where?
**donut m** doughnut
**dormir** sleep
**dos veces** twice
**droga f** drug (narcotic)
**droga mitigadora**
painkiller
**droga tranquilizante**
tranquillizer

**ducha f** shower
**duele** it hurts
**dueño/a m/f** owner
**dulce** sweet (adj)
**dulce m** candy
**durante** during
**durante la noche**
overnight
**duro/a** hard, tough

**E**
**echar** throw
**echar de menos**
homesickness
**economía f** economy
**edad f** age
**edificio m** building
**edificio de aparta-**
**mentos** block of flats
**edredón m** duvet, quilt
**educado/a** formal,
polite
**efectivo** cash
**ejemplo m** example
**él** he, him
**él/ella/ello** it (subject)
**el/los** the
**el piso más alto**
top floor
**elástico/a** elastic
**electricidad f** electricity
**electricista m/f**
electrician
**eléctrico/a** electric
**elegante** posh
**elegir** choose
**elevador** lift, elevator

**SPANISH → ENGLISH**

**elevador de silla**
chair lift
**ella** she
**ellos/ellas** they
**embajada f** embassy
**embarazada** pregnant
**embotellamiento m**
traffic jam
**embrague m**
clutch (car)
**emergencia f**
emergency
**empacar** pack (vb)
**empanada f** pie
**empaste m**
filling (tooth)
**empezar** start
**empinado/a** steep
**empujar** push
**en** at, in, into, on
**en algún lugar**
somewhere
**en el extranjero**
abroad
**en forma** fit (healthy)
**en los alrededores**
nearby
**en lugar de** instead
**¡Encantado!**
Pleased to meet you!
**encantado/a** glad
**encendedor m**
cigarette lighter
**encender** switch on
**encendido m** ignition
**enchufe m** plug,
socket (elec)
**encoger** shrink

**encontrar** find, meet
**enero m** January
**enfadado** angry
**enfermedad f** disease,
illness
**enfermedad de
trasmisión sexual**
venereal disease
**enfermero/a m/f**
nurse
**enfermo/a** ill, sick
**¡Enhorabuena!**
Congratulations!
**enojado** angry
**ensalada f** salad
**enseñar** teach
**ensuciar** litter (vb)
**entender** understand
**entero/a** whole (adj)
**entrada f** admission
fee, cover charge,
entrance, entrance fee
**entrar** enter
**entre** come in
**entrega f** delivery
**entregar** deliver
**entusiasmante**
exciting
**enviar** send
**enviar por correo**
mail, post (vb)
**envolver** wrap up
**epilepsia f** epilepsy
**epiléptico/a** epileptic
**equipaje m** baggage,
luggage
**equipaje de mano**
hand luggage

EST

**equipo** m equipment, gear, team
**era/estaba** were
**error** m error, mistake
**erupción** f rash
**es/está** is
**escalera** f ladder, stairs
**escalera mecánica** escalator
**escalfado** poached
**escalón** m step
**escapar** escape (vb)
**escarbadientes** toothpick
**escayola** f plaster
**escoba** f broom
**escocés/escocesa** m/f Scot, Scottish (n, adj)
**Escocia** Scotland
**escoger** choose
**esconder** hide
**escribir** write
**escritorio** m desk
**escuchar** hear, listen
**escuela** f school
**ese/esa** m/f that
**esencial** essential
**eslovaco** Slovak
**esmalte de uñas** nail varnish/polish
**esos/esas** those
**espalda** f back
**España** Spain
**español/a** m/f Spaniard, Spanish
**esparadrapo** m sticking plaster

**especia** f spice
**especialidad** f speciality
**especialmente** especially
**espectáculo** m show (n)
**espectáculo de marionetas** puppet show
**espejo** m mirror
**espejo retrovisor** rear-view mirror
**esperanza** f hope
**esperar** expect, wait
**esperar con ilusión** look forward to
**espina** f thorn
**espinacas** fpl spinach
**espinazo** m spine
**espiral** f coil (n, contraceptive)
**espíritu** m spirit
**esponja** f sponge
**esposa** f wife
**esposo** m husband
**esquí** m ski (n)
**esquí acuático** water-skiing
**esquiar** ski (vb)
**esquina** f corner
**está bien** all right
**esta mañana** this morning
**esta noche** tonight
**esta semana** this week
**estaca** f tent peg
**estación** f station

SPANISH → ENGLISH

SPANISH → ENGLISH

**estación de ferrocarril/tren** railway station
**estación de policía** police station
**estación de servicio** petrol station
**estadio** m stadium
**Estados Unidos** United States
**estafa** f rip-off
**estampilla** f stamp, postage stamp
**están** are
**estante** m shelf
**estar** be
**estar de acuerdo** agree
**estatua** f statue
**este** m east
**este/esta** this
**estómago** m stomach
**Estonia** Estonia
**estornudar** sneeze
**estrecho/a** narrow
**estrella** f star
**estreñido/a** constipated
**estudiante** m/f student
**estufilla** f gas cooker
**estúpido/a** stupid
**etiqueta** f label, luggage tag
**Europa** Europe
**europeo/a** European (adj, n)
**evitar** avoid
**exactamente** exactly

**exacto** accurate
**examen** m examination
**excelente** excellent
**excepto** except
**exceso de equipaje** excess luggage
**excluir** exclude
**excursión** f excursion
**experimentado/a** experienced
**explicar** explain
**explosión** f explosion
**explotar** burst
**exportar** export
**exposición** f exhibition, exposure
**expreso** m express (train)
**extensión** f extension
**extintor de fuego** fire extinguisher
**extra** extra
**extranjero/a** m/f foreign, foreigner (adj, n)
**extraño/a** m/f strange, stranger (adj, n)
**extraordinario/a** extraordinary

**F**
**fábrica** f factory
**fábrica de cerveza** brewery
**fabuloso** amazing
**fachada** f façade
**fácil** easy
**facsímil** fax
**factura** f invoice

**falda** f skirt
**falso/a** fake (adj), false
**familia** f family
**famoso/a** famous
**farmacéutico/a** m/f
chemist, pharmacist
**farmacia** f pharmacy
**faro** m headlight
**fascinante** astonishing
**favorito/a** favourite
**febrero** m February
**fecha** f date (of year)
**fecha de nacimiento**
date of birth
**fecha de vencimiento**
sell-by date
**felicitaciones** fpl
congratulations
**feliz** happy
**¡Feliz Año Nuevo!**
Happy New Year!
**¡Feliz Semana Santa!**
Happy Easter!
**feo/a** ugly, awful
**feria** f fair (fête)
**ferretería** f DIY shop,
hardware shop,
ironmonger's
**ferrocarril** m railway
**ferry** m ferry
**festival** m festival
**fibra sintética**
man-made fibre
**fiebre** f fever
**fiebre del heno**
hay fever
**fiesta** f party
(celebration)

**fiesta nacional**
public holiday
**fila** f row (n)
**filete** m fillet
**film a color** colour film
**filmar** film (vb)
**filtro** m filter
**fin de semana**
weekend
**final** m end
**finalmente** eventually
**fino/a** fine (adj)
**firma** f signature
**firmar** sign (vb)
**flaco/a** thin
**flor** f flower
**florista** m/f florist
**folleto** m brochure,
leaflet
**fontanero/a** m/f
plumber
**forma** f form (shape)
**formal** formal
**formulario** m form
(document)
**formulario de**
**inscripción**
registration form
**fósforos** mpl
matches (for lighting)
**foto** f photo, picture
**fotocopia** f
photocopy (n)
**fotografía** f
photograph (n)
**fotografiar**
photograph (vb)
**fractura** f fracture

SPANISH → ENGLISH

**frágil** breakable
**frambuesa f** raspberry
**francés/francesa m/f** French, Frenchman/woman (adj, n)
**Francia** France
**franela f** flannel
**franqueo m** postage
**frasco m** jar
**frase f** sentence (grammar)
**frecuente** frequent
**fregadero m** sink
**freír** fry
**freno m** brake (n)
**freno de mano** handbrake
**frente f** forehead
**frente m** front
**fresa f** strawberry
**fresco/a** cool, fresh
**frijol m** bean
**frío/a** cold
**frito/a** fried
**fruta f** fruit
**frutilla f** strawberry
**fuego m** fire
**fuente f** fountain
**fuera** away, out, outside
**fuerte** strong, tough
**fuerte m** fortress
**fumar** smoke (vb)
**funda para almohada** pillowcase
**funda para edredón** duvet cover
**funeral m** funeral

**funicular m** funicular
**furúnculo m** boil (n)
**fusible m** fuse
**fútbol m** football
**futuro m** future

**G**
**gafas fpl** glasses, spectacles
**gafas de sol** sunglasses
**gafas protectoras** goggles
**galería f** gallery
**Gales** Wales
**galés/galesa m/f** Welsh, Welshman, Welshwoman (adj, n)
**galleta f** biscuit, cookie
**galón m** gallon
**gamba f** prawn
**gamuza f** suede
**ganar** win
**ganso m** goose
**garaje m** garage
**garantía f** guarantee
**garganta f** throat
**gas m** gas
**gasolina f** petrol, fuel
**gasolinera f** petrol station
**gastar** spend (money)
**gastos mpl** expenses
**gato m** jack (car)
**gato/a m/f** cat
**gaviota f** seagull
**gay** gay
**gemelos** twins

**gemelos** mpl  cufflinks
**general**  general
**generalmente**  mostly, usually
**generoso/a**  generous
**gente** f  folk, people
**genuino/a**  genuine
**gerente** m/f  manager
**gimnasio** m  gym
**Ginebra**  Geneva
**giro** m  money order
**glaciar** m  glacier
**gobierno** m  government
**golpear**  hit, knock
**goma** f  rubber
**goma de mascar**  chewing gum
**gordo/a**  fat
**gorro** m  cap
**gota** f  drop (n)
**gotas para los ojos**  eye drops
**gotear**  leak (vb)
**gótico/a**  Gothic
**grabadora** f  tape recorder
**gracioso/a**  funny
**grado**  degree (measurement)
**gradualmente**  gradually
**gramática** f  grammar
**gramo** m  gram
**gran, grande**  great, big, large
**Gran Bretaña**  Great Britain

**grandes almacenes** mpl  department store
**grandioso/a**  grand
**granero** m  barn
**granizo** m  hail
**granja** f  farm
**granjero/a** m/f  farmer
**grapar**  staple
**graso/a**  fatty, greasy
**Grecia**  Greece
**griego/a** m/f  Greek (adj, n)
**gripe** f  flu
**gris**  grey
**gritar**  shout (vb)
**grito** m  shout (n)
**grosella negra**  blackcurrant
**grosella roja**  redcurrant
**grueso/a**  thick
**grupo** m  group
**guantes** mpl  gloves
**guapo/a**  handsome
**guardabarros** m  bumper, fender
**guardar**  keep
**guardar en el armario**  lock in
**guardarropa** m  wardrobe
**¡Guarde el cambio!**  Keep the change!
**guardería de niños**  crèche
**guardería infantil**  nursery school
**guardia** m/f  guard

**guardia costera** coastguard
**guardia de seguridad** security guard
**guerra f** war
**guía m/f** guide
**guía de turismo** guide book, tour guide
**guía telefónica** telephone directory
**guisante m** pea
**guiso m** stew
**guitarra f** guitar
**gusano m** maggot
**gustar** like (vb)
**gusto m** taste

## H
**haba f** bean
**habitación f** room
**habitación doble** double room
**habitación libre** vacancy
**habitación para uno/single** single room
**hablar** speak, talk
**hace una semana** a week ago
**hacer** do, make
**hacer autostop** hitchhike
**hacer cola** queue (vb)
**hacer dedo** hitchhike
**hacienda f** farmhouse
**hamburguesa f** hamburger

**harina f** flour
**hasta** even (adv), till, until
**¿Hay algo mal/malo?** What is wrong?
**hecho/a** made
**hecho a mano** handmade
**helada f** frost
**helado m** ice cream
**helicóptero m** helicopter
**herida f** injury
**herido/a** injured
**hermana f** sister
**hermano m** brother
**hernia f** hernia
**herpes m** shingles
**herramienta f** tool
**hervidor m** kettle
**hervir** boil (vb)
**hidroala f** hydrofoil
**hidrodeslizador m** hovercraft
**hielo m** ice
**hierbas fpl** herbs
**hierro m** iron (n, metal)
**hígado m** liver
**hija f** daughter
**hijo m** son
**hilado m** thread
**hilo dental** dental floss
**hinchado/a** swollen
**hincharse** swell
**hinchazón f** swelling
**hipódromo m** race course
**historia f** history
**histórico/a** historic

**hoja** f leaf
**hoja de afeitar** razor blade
**hoja de laurel** bay leaf
**holandés/holandesa** m/f Dutch, Dutchman, Dutchwoman (adj, n)
**hombre** m man
**hombres** men
**hombro** m shoulder
**homosexual** gay, homosexual
**hongo** m mushroom
**honrado/a** honest
**hora** f hour, time
**horario** m timetable
**horario de apertura** opening times
**horario de visita** visiting hours
**hormiga** ant
**hornalla** f gas cooker
**hornillo** m cooker
**horno** m oven
**horrible** dreadful
**hospital** m hospital
**hospitalidad** f hospitality
**hoy** m today
**hoyo** m hole
**hueco** m hole
**huelga** f strike (n)
**hueso** m bone
**huésped/a** m/f guest
**huevo** m egg
**huevo de Pascua** Easter egg

**huevos revueltos** scrambled eggs
**humedad** f damp (n)
**húmedo/a** humid
**humita** bow tie
**humo** m smoke (n)
**humor** m humour
**húngaro/a** m/f Hungarian (adj, n)
**Hungría** Hungary

**I**

**ictericia** f jaundice
**idea** f idea
**idioma** m language
**iglesia** f church
**igual** same (adv)
**ilimitado/a** unlimited
**iluminar** light (vb)
**imán** m magnet
**impar** odd (number)
**imperdible** m safety pin
**imperfección** f flaw
**impermeable** m raincoat
**importante** great, important
**imposible** impossible
**impresos** mpl printed matter
**imprimir** print (vb)
**impuesto** m tax
**Impuesto sobre Valor Añadido** Value Added Tax
**incluido** included
**incómodo/a** uncomfortable

SPANISH → ENGLISH

SPANISH → ENGLISH

**inconciente**
unconscious
**inconveniente f**
inconvenience
**increíble** incredible
**indecente** nasty
**independiente**
freelance
**indicador de giro**
indicator
**indicador de la
gasolina** fuel gauge
**indigestión f**
indigestion
**indio/a m/f** Indian
(adj, n)
**infección f** infection
**infeccioso/a** infectious
**inflamación f**
inflammation
**inflar** pump, inflate
**información f**
information
**informal** informal
**informar** report (vb)
**informe m** enquiry,
report (n)
**ingeniero/a m/f**
engineer
**Inglaterra** England
**inglés** English
(language)
**inglés/inglesa m/f**
English, Englishman/
woman (adj, n)
**ingredientes mpl**
ingredients

**inmediatamente**
immediately
**inscribirse** check in
**insecto m** insect
**insistir** insist
**insolación f** sunstroke
**insólito/a** unusual
**insomnio m** insomnia
**instalación f**
connection (telephone)
**insulina f** insulin
**inteligente** clever,
intelligent
**intentar** try
**intercambio m**
exchange (n)
**interesante** interesting
**intermitente m**
indicator
**internacional**
international
**intérprete m/f**
interpreter
**interruptor m** switch
**interruptor principal**
mains switch
**intervalo m** interval
**introducir** introduce,
bring in
**inundación f** flood
**inválido/a** disabled
**investigación f** enquiry,
investigation
**invierno m** winter
**invitación f** invitation
**invitar** invite
**inyección f** injection
**ir** go

**ir conducir/manejar**
go (by car)
**Irlanda** Ireland
**Irlanda del Norte**
Northern Ireland
**irlandés/irlandesa m/f**
Irish, Irishman/woman
(adj, n)
**irse** go away
**isla f** island
**Italia** Italy
**italiano m** Italian
(language)
**italiano/a m/f** Italian
(adj, n)
**IVA** VAT
**izquierdo/a** left

**J**
**jabalí m** boar
**jabón m** soap
**jabón en polvo** soap
powder
**jalea f** jelly, jam
**jamón m** ham
**jarabe para la tos**
cough mixture
**jardín m** garden
**jardín de infancia**
nursery school
**jardín zoológico** zoo
**jarra f** jug
**jersey m** jersey, jumper,
pullover
**jóven** young
**joyas fpl** jewellery
**joyería f** jeweller's

**jubilado/a m/f** old-age
pensioner, senior citizen
**jubilado/a** retired
**judía f** bean
**judío/a m/f** Jewish, Jew
(adj, n)
**juego m** game
**juego de fútbol**
football match
**jueves m** Thursday
**juez m/f** judge
**jugar** play (vb, game)
**jugo m** juice
**jugo de fruta** fruit juice
**jugo de naranja**
orange juice
**jugo de tomate**
tomato juice
**juguete m** toy
**julio m** July
**junio m** June
**junto a** beside
**juntos/as** together
**juntura f** joint
**jurar** swear (an oath)
**justo/a** fair, just

**K**
**kilo m** kilo
**kilogramo m** kilogram
**kilómetro m** kilometre

**L**
**la/las** the
**la mayoría de** most
**la semana pasada**
a week ago
**lado m** side

SPANISH → ENGLISH

**ladrar** bark (vb)
**ladrillo** m brick
**ladrón/ladrona** m/f
 thief, burglar
**lago** m lake
**lámpara** f lamp
**lamparilla** f light bulb
**lana** f wool
**lancha** f motorboat
**lancha neumática**
 dinghy
**langosta** f lobster
**lapicera** pen, ballpoint
 pen
**lápiz** m pencil
**lápiz de labios** lipstick
**largo/a** long (size)
**lastimado/a** injured
**lata** f can (n), tin
**Latvia** Latvia
**lavabo** m washbasin
**lavado de coches**
 car wash
**lavandería** f laundry
**lavandería automática**
 launderette, laundromat
**lavaplatos** m
 dishwasher
**lavar** wash
**lavar y marcar**
 shampoo and set
**laxante** m laxative
 (adj, n)
**le** it (indirect object)
**lección** f lesson
**leche** f milk
**leche en polvo**
 powdered milk

**lechuga** f lettuce
**lechuza** f owl
**leer** read
**lejano/a** far (adj)
**lejos** far (adv)
**lengua** f language,
 tongue
**lenguado** m sole (fish)
**lente** f lens
**lenteja** f lentil
**lentes** m/f glasses,
 spectacles, lenses
**lentes de contacto**
 contact lenses
**lento/a** slow
**león** m lion
**lesbiana** f lesbian
 (adj, n)
**levantar** lift (vb)
**levantarse** get up
**ley** f law
**libra** f pound
**libre** free
**libre de impuestos**
 duty-free
**librería** f bookshop
**libreta de cheques**
 cheque book
**libro** m book
**libro de frases** phrase
 book
**licencia** f licence
**licencia de conductor**
 driving licence
**licor** m liqueur
**licores** mpl spirits
 (drink)
**liebre** f hare

SPANISH → ENGLISH

**ligero/a** light (adj, weight)
**lima f** file (tool), lime
**lima de uñas** nailfile
**límite de velocidad** speed limit
**limón m** lemon
**limonada f** lemonade
**limpiaparabrisas m** windscreen wiper
**limpiar** clean (vb)
**limpio/a** clean (adj)
**lindo/a** beautiful
**línea f** line
**lino m** linen
**linterna f** torch
**linterna eléctrica** flashlight
**líquido de freno** brake fluid
**líquido para lavar** washing-up liquid
**liquído para remojar** soaking solution
**lista f** list
**listo/a** clever, ready
**litera f** couchette
**litro m** litre
**Lituania** Lithuania
**liviano/a** light (adj, weight)
**llamada f** call (n)
**llamada a cobro revertido** collect call, reverse-charge call
**llamada de larga distancia** long-distance call

**llamada para despertar** wake-up call
**llamada telefónica** telephone call
**llamar** call (vb)
**llave f** key, spanner
**llave de contacto/ encendido** ignition key
**llave de tuercas** spanner
**llavero m** key ring
**llaves del coche** car keys
**llegada f** arrival
**llegar** arrive
**llenar** fill, fill in, fill up
**lleno/a** crowded, full, stuffed
**llevar** lead (vb), wear
**llorar** cry
**lluvia f** rain
**lo/la** it (direct object)
**¡Lo siento!** Sorry!
**lobo m** wolf
**local** local
**loco/a** mad, crazy
**lodo m** mud
**los dos** both
**loza f** crockery
**luces delanteras** headlights
**lucha f** fight (n)
**luchar** fight (vb)
**luego** afterwards, later
**lugar m** place
**lujo m** luxury

SPANISH → ENGLISH

169

SPANISH → ENGLISH

**luna** f  moon
**luna de miel**
  honeymoon
**lunes** m  Monday
**lupa** f  magnifying glass
**Luxemburgo**
  Luxembourg
**luz** f  light (n)
**luz de freno**  brake light
**luz del sol**  sunshine

**M**
**madera** f  wood
**madrastra** f
  stepmother
**madre** f  mother
**maduro/a**  ripe
**maestro/a** m/f  teacher
**magdalena** f  bun
**malentendido** m
  misunderstanding
**maleta** f  suitcase
**maletero** m  boot,
  trunk (car)
**maletín** m  briefcase
**maletín de primeros
  auxilios**  first-aid kit
**malo/a**  awful, mean,
  bad, nasty, poor (quality)
**mancha** f  stain
**mandíbula** f  jaw
**manejar**  drive
**mango** m  handle
**manguera** f  hose pipe
**maní** m  peanut
**mano** f  hand
**manojo** m  bunch
**manta** f  blanket

**mantel** m  tablecloth
**mantequilla** f  butter
**manual** m  manual
  (adj, n)
**mañana** f  morning
**mañana** m  tomorrow
**mañana por la
  mañana/tarde/
  noche**  tomorrow
  morning/afternoon/
  evening
**mapa** m  map
**mapa de calles**
  street map
**mapa de carreteras**
  road map
**máquina** f  machine
**máquina expendedora**
  vending machine
**mar** m/f  sea
**Mar Báltico**  Baltic Sea
**Mar del Norte**  North
  Sea
**maravilloso**  amazing
**marca** f  brand
**marcapasos** m
  pacemaker
**marcar**  dial (vb)
**marcha atrás**  reverse
  gear
**marco** m  frame
**marco de foto**  picture
  frame
**marea** f  tide
**marea alta**  high tide
**marea baja**  low tide
**mareado/a**  dizzy,
  seasick

**mareo m** travel sickness

**marido m** husband

**mariposa f** butterfly

**mariscos mpl** shellfish

**mármol m** marble

**marrón** brown

**martillo m** hammer

**marzo m** March

**más** more

**más allá** beyond, further

**más barato** cheaper

**más tarde** later

**máscara f** mask

**masculino** male

**mástil m** mast

**matar** kill

**matrícula f** number plate

**mayo m** May

**mayonesa f** mayonnaise

**me** me

**mecánico/a m/f** mechanic

**mechero m** cigarette lighter

**media f** stocking

**mediano/a** medium

**medianoche f** midnight

**medias fpl** socks, tights

**medicamento m** drug, medicine

**medicina f** medicine (science)

**médico/a m/f** doctor

**medida f** measure (n)

**medieval** medieval

**medio m** middle

**medio/a** half (adj)

**mediodía m** midday, noon

**medir** measure (vb)

**mediterráneo/a** Mediterranean

**medusa f** jellyfish

**mejilla f** cheek

**mejillón m** mussel

**mejor** better

**mejorar** improve

**melocotón m** peach

**melón m** melon

**mencionar** mention

**meningitis** meningitis

**menos** less

**mensualmente** monthly

**menta f** mint

**mente f** mind

**mentir** lie (vb, fib)

**mentira f** lie (n, untruth)

**mentón m** chin

**menú m** menu

**menú fijo** set menu

**mercado m** market

**merengue m** meringue

**mermelada f** jam, marmalade

**mes m** month

**mesa f** table

**metal m** metal

**metro m** metre, metro, subway, underground

**mezclar** mix

**mezquita f** mosque

SPANISH → ENGLISH

171

**mi** my
**micro ondas** m
　microwave oven
**miel** f honey
**mientras** while
**miércoles** m
　Wednesday
**migraña** f migraine
**mil** m thousand
**milla** f mile
**ministro/a** m/f minister
**minúsculo/a** tiny
**minusválido/a**
　handicapped
**minuto** m minute (n)
**miope** short-sighted
**mirar** look at, watch (vb)
**misa** f Mass (rel)
**mismo/a** same (adj)
**mitad** f half (n)
**mitigador** painkiller
**mochila** f backpack
**mojado/a** wet
**molestar** annoy, disturb
**momento** m moment
**monasterio** m
　monastery
**moneda** f coin,
　currency
**monedero** m money
　belt, purse
**montaña** f mountain
**montañismo** m
　mountaineering
**montar** ride
**montar en bicicleta**
　cycle (vb)
**monto** m amount

**monumento** m
　monument
**morado** m bruise (n)
**morado/a** purple
**morder** bite (vb)
**morir** die
**mosquito** m mosquito
**mostaza** f mustard
**mostrador** m counter
**mostrador de**
　**información**
　enquiry desk
**mostrar** show (vb)
**motocicleta** f
　motorbike
**motor** m engine, motor
**mover** move
**mozo/a** m/f waiter,
　waitress
**muchedumbre** f
　crowd
**mucho/a** long (time), lot,
　much
**muchos/muchas**
　many
**mudarse de casa**
　move house
**muebles** mpl furniture
**muelle** m quay
**muerte** f death
**muerto/a** dead
**mugriento/a** filthy
**mujer** f female, lady,
　woman
**muletas** fpl crutches
**multa** f fine (n)
**mundo** m world
**muñeca** f doll, wrist

SPANISH → ENGLISH

**muro** m  wall
**músculo** m  muscle
**museo** m  museum
**músico/a** m/f  musician
**muslo** m  thigh
**musulmán/
   musulmana** m/f
   Muslim
**muy**  very
**muy hecho**  overdone

# N

**nacer**  born
**nacimiento** m  birth
**nacional**  national
**nacionalidad** f
   nationality
**nada**  nothing
**nada más**  nothing else
**nadar**  swim
**nadie**  nobody
**naranja** f  orange
**nariz** f  nose
**nata montada**
   whipped cream
**natillas** fpl  custard
**natural**  natural
**naturaleza** f  nature
**náusea** f  nausea
**navaja de afeitar**
   razor
**navegación** f  sailing
**navegar**  sail
**Navidad** f  Christmas
**neblina** f  fog, mist
**necesario/a**  necessary
**necesidad** f  need (n)
**necesitar**  need (vb)

**negativo** m  negative
   (n, photo)
**negocios** mpl  business
**negro/a**  black
**neocelandés**  New
   Zealander
**neumático** m  tyre
**neumático de
   repuesto**  spare tyre
**neumático sin aire**
   flat tyre
**nevera** f  fridge
**nevera portátil**  cool
   bag, cool box
**ni ... ni**  neither ... nor
**nido** m  nest
**niebla** f  fog
**nieta** f  granddaughter
**nieto** m  grandson
**nieve, está nevando**
   snow, it is snowing
**ninguno/a**  none
**niña** f  girl
**niñera** f  nanny
**niño** m  boy
**niño/a** m/f  child
**no**  no, not
**no contiene azúcar**
   sugar-free
**no fumador/a**  non-
   smoking
**no funciona**  out of
   order
**no importa**  it doesn't
   matter
**no puedo**  couldn't
**noche** f  late evening,
   night

SPANISH → ENGLISH

**Nochebuena** f
  Christmas Eve
**Nochevieja** f New
  Year's Eve
**nombre** m name
**nombre de pila**
  Christian name, first
  name
**nombre de soltera**
  maiden name
**norte** m north
**Noruega** Norway
**noruego/a** m/f
  Norwegian (adj, n)
**nos** us
**nosotros/as** us, we
**nota** f note
**noticias** fpl news
**novela** f novel
**novia** f bride, fiancée,
  girlfriend
**noviembre** m
  November
**novio** m bridegroom,
  fiancé, boyfriend
**nube** f cloud
**nuera** f daughter-in-law
**nuestro/a** our
**Nueva Zelanda** New
  Zealand
**nuevo/a** new
**nuez** f nut, walnut
**número** m number, size
**número de clave**
  pin number
**número de
  inscripción**
  registration number

**número de teléfono**
  phone number
**nunca** never

**O**
**o** or
**o ... o** either ... or
**obligatorio/a**
  compulsory
**obra** f play (n, theatre)
**obtener** get, obtain
**océano** m ocean
**octubre** m October
**oculista** m/f
  ophthalmologist
**ocupación** f occupation
**ocupado/a** busy,
  engaged, occupied
**oeste** m west
**oficina** f office
**oficina de cambio**
  bureau de change
**oficina de correos**
  post office
**oído** m ear
**oír** hear
**ojalá** hopefully
**ojo** m eye
**ojotas** fpl sandals
**ola** f wave
**oler** smell
**olvidar** forget
**ópera** f opera
**operación** f operation
**operador/a** m/f
  operator (phone)
**operador de turismo**
  tour operator

**oporto** m  port (wine)
**óptico/a** m/f  optician
**opuesto/a**  opposite
**orden** m  order (n)
**ordenador** m
  computer
**orilla** f  hem, shore
**oro** m  gold
**orquesta** f  orchestra
**oscuro/a**  dark
**otoño** m  autumn
**otra vez**  again
**otro/a**  other, another
**oveja** f  sheep
**oxidado/a**  rusty

**P**

**paciente** m/f  patient
  (adj, n)
**padrastro** m  stepfather
**padre** m  father
**padres** mpl  parents
**pagadero/a**  due
**pagado/a**  paid
**pagar**  pay
**página** f  page
**páginas amarillas**
  yellow pages
**pago** m  payment
**país** m  country
**paisaje** m  scenery
**Países Bajos**
  Netherlands
**paja** f  straw
**pajarita** f  bow tie
**pájaro** m  bird
**pala** f  spade
**palabra** f  word

**palabrota** f  swear-word
**palacio** m  palace
**palanca** f  handle, lever
**palanca de cambios**
  gear lever
**pálido/a**  pale
**palo de golf**  golf club
  (stick)
**pan** m  bread
**pan de centeno**  rye
  bread
**pan integral de trigo**
  wholemeal bread
**panadería** f  bakery
**pantalla** f  screen
**pantalones** mpl  pants,
  trousers
**pantalones cortos**
  mpl  shorts
**pantano** m  marsh
**panty** m  pantyhose
**pañal** m  diaper, nappy
**pañales descartables**
  disposable diapers/
  nappies
**paño** m  cloth, duster
**paño para el suelo**
  floorcloth
**pañuelo** m
  handkerchief
**papa** f  potato
**papas fritas** fpl  chips,
  crisps, French fries
**papel** m  paper
**papel de carta**
  notepaper
**papel de envolver**
  wrapping paper

SPANISH → ENGLISH

**papel de escribir**
writing paper
**papel metálico** tinfoil
**papelería f** stationer's
**paperas fpl** mumps
**paquete m** package,
packet, parcel
**par m** pair
**para** for (purpose)
**parabrisas m**
windscreen
**parachoques m**
fender
**parada f** stopover
**parada de autobús**
bus stop
**parada de taxis** taxi
rank
**parador m** hostel
**paraguas m** umbrella
**parar** stay, stop
**pardo/a** brown
**pare** stop sign
**parecido/a** similar
**pared f** wall
**pareja f** couple
**parejo/a** even (adj)
**pariente m/f** relative,
relation
**parque m** park (n)
**parquímetro m** parking
meter
**parte f** part, portion
**parte de arriba** top
**parte de repuesto**
spare part
**partes del coche** car
parts

**partido m** match
(sport), party (political)
**partido de fútbol**
football match
**pasa f** raisin
**pasado m** past
**pasado/a de moda**
old-fashioned
**pasajero/a m/f**
passenger
**pasaporte m** passport
**pasar** happen, pass,
spend (time)
**paseo a caballo** horse
riding
**pasillo m** aisle, corridor
**paso de peatones**
pedestrian crossing
**pastel m** cake, pastry,
pie
**pastelería f** cake shop
**pastilla f** pill
**pastilla para dormir**
sleeping pill
**pastillas para la
garganta** throat
lozenges
**patata f** potato
**patatas fritas fpl**
chips, crisps, French
fries
**patear** kick
**patín m** skate (n)
**patinar** skate (vb)
**patines mpl** ice skates
**patio de recreo**
playground
**pato/a m/f** duck

**patrón** m pattern
**pavo** m turkey
**peaje** m toll
**peatón** m pedestrian
**pecho** m breast, chest
**peculiar** peculiar
**pedal** m pedal
**pedazo** m piece
**pedido** m request (n)
**pedir** order, request (vb)
**pegado** stuck
**pegamento** m glue
**pegar** stick (vb)
**peinar** comb (vb)
**peine** m comb (n)
**pelar** peel (vb)
**pelea** f fight (n)
**pelear** fight, quarrel (vb)
**película** f film (n)
**peligro** m danger
**peligroso/a** dangerous
**pelo** m hair
**peluca** f wig
**peluquería** f
  hairdresser's
**peluquero/a** m/f
  hairdresser
**pena** f pity
**pendientes** mpl
  earrings
**península** f peninsula
**pensar** think
**pensión** f bed &
  breakfast, boarding
  house, guesthouse
**pensión completa** full
  board
**peor** worse

**pepino** m cucumber
**pequeño/a** little, small
**pera** f pear
**percha** f hanger
**percha para abrigo**
  coat hanger
**perder** lose
**perdido/a** lost, missing
**¡Perdón!** Excuse me!
**perezoso/a** lazy
**perfecto/a** perfect
**perfume** m perfume
**periódico** m
  newspaper
**período** m period
**perla** f pearl
**permanente** f perm
**permiso** m licence,
  permit (n)
**permiso de caza**
  hunting permit
**permiso de pesca**
  fishing permit
**permitir** let, allow,
  permit (vb)
**pero** but
**perro/a** m/f dog
**persiana** blind (n)
**persona** f person
**pesado/a** dull, boring,
  heavy
**pesar** weigh
**pescadería** f
  fishmonger's
**pescado** m fish
**peso** m weight
**petición** f request (n)
**piano** m piano

SPANISH → ENGLISH

SPANISH → ENGLISH

**picadura** f  sting (n)
**picadura de insecto**
  insect bite
**picar**  itch, sting (vb)
**picnic** m  picnic
**pico** m  peak
**picor** m  itch (n)
**pie** m  foot
**piedra** f  stone
**piel** f  fur, leather, peel,
  skin
**pierna** f  leg
**pies** mpl  feet
**pieza** f  piece
**pijamas** m  pyjamas
**piloto** m  pilot
**pimienta** f  pepper
  (spice)
**pimiento** m  pepper
  (vegetable)
**pinchazo** m  puncture
**pintar**  paint (vb)
**pintura** f  paint (n)
**pintura de uñas**  nail
  varnish/polish
**pinza** f  clothes peg
**pinzas** fpl  tweezers
**piña** f  pineapple
**pipa** f  pipe (smoking)
**pirulí** m  lollipop
**piscina** f  pool
**piscina climatizada/
  cubierta**  indoor pool
**piso** m  apartment, flat,
  floor, storey
**pista de hielo**  ice rink
**pista de patinaje**
  skating rink

**pista de tenis**  tennis
  court
**pista para esquiar**  ski
  slope
**pistas para
  principiantes**
  nursery slope
**plancha** f  iron
  (n, appliance)
**planchar**  iron (vb)
**planta** f  plant, storey
**planta baja**  ground
  floor
**plástico/a**  plastic
**plástico para envolver**
  cling film
**plata** f  silver
**plataforma** f  platform
**platillo** m  saucer
**platinos** mpl  points
  (car)
**plato** m  dish, plate
**plato principal**  main
  course
**playa** f  beach
**playa nudista**  nudist
  beach
**plaza** f  square
**plomero/a** m  plumber
**plomo** m  lead (n, metal)
**población** f  population
**pobre**  poor
  (impecunious)
**pocillo** m  cup
**poco a poco**  gradually
**poco hecho**
  underdone

**poco profundo/a** shallow
**pocos/pocas** m/f few, a few
**poder** can (vb), may, might
**¿Podría?** Could I?
**podrido/a** rotten
**polaco/a** m/f Polish, Pole (adj, n)
**policía** f police
**polilla** f moth
**pollo** m chicken
**Polonia** Poland
**polvo** m dust, powder
**polvo de lavar** washing powder
**pomada** f ointment
**poner** put
**popular** popular
**por** by, for, because of, per, through, via
**por adelantado** in advance
**por aquí** this way
**por ejemplo** for example
**por favor** please
**por horas** hourly (adv)
**por la mañana** a.m. (before noon)
**por la noche** overnight
**por la tarde** p.m. (after noon)
**¿Por qué?** Why?
**por su cuenta** freelance
**por suerte** fortunately

**por supuesto** absolutely, definitely
**por todas partes** everywhere
**porcelana** f china
**porción** f portion
**porque** because
**portaequipaje** m luggage rack, roof-rack
**portero** m doorman
**portero/a** m/f caretaker, porter
**Portugal** Portugal
**portugués/ portuguesa** m/f Portuguese (adj, n)
**posada** f inn
**posible** possible
**postal** f postcard
**poste indicador** signpost
**póster** m poster
**postre** m dessert, pudding
**práctica** f practice
**practicar** practise
**precio** m price
**precio barato** cheap rate
**precio de temporada alta** peak rate
**precioso/a** beautiful, lovely
**preferir** prefer
**prefijo** m dialling code
**pregunta** f question
**preguntar** ask
**premio** m prize

**preocupado/a** worried
**presentar** introduce
  (people)
**presente** present (adj)
**preservativo** m
  condom
**presión** f pressure
**presión alta (sangre)**
  high blood pressure
**presión arterial** blood
  pressure
**presión en los
  neumáticos** tyre
  pressure
**prestar** lend
**primavera** f spring
  (season)
**primer nombre** first
  name
**primer piso** m first floor
**primer/a ministro/a**
  m/f prime minister
**primera clase** first
  class
**primero/a** first
**primeros auxilios**
  first aid
**primo/a** m/f cousin
**principal** main
**principiante** m/f
  beginner
**prismáticos** mpl
  binoculars
**privado/a** private
**probablemente**
  probably
**probarse** try on
**problema** m problem

**problemas** mpl trouble
**profesor/a** m/f teacher
**profundo/a** deep
**programa** m
  programme, program
**prohibido/a** forbidden,
  prohibited
**promedio** average
**promesa** f promise (n)
**prometer** promise (vb)
**prometido/a** m/f
  fiancé, fiancée
**pronóstico del tiempo**
  weather forecast
**pronto** soon
**pronunciar** pronounce
**propiedad perdida**
  lost property
**propietario/a** m/f
  landlord/landlady,
  owner
**propina** f service
  charge, tip, gratuity
**protestante** m/f
  Protestant
**próximo/a** next
**público/a** public
**pueblo** m village
**¿Puedo?** Could I?
**puente** m bridge
**puerco** m/f pig
**puerro** m leek
**puerta** f door, gate
**puerto** m port, harbour
**puesto** m stall
**pulga** f flea
**pulgada** f inch
**pulgar** m thumb

SPANISH → ENGLISH

**pulir** polish (vb)
**pulmón** m lung
**pulsera** f bracelet
**puntada** f stitch
**puntilla** f lace
**punto** m point (n)
**puré de papas/
  patatas** mashed
  potatoes
**puro** m cigar

## Q

**¿Qué?** Pardon? What?
**que hace juego**
  matching
**¿Qué hora es?** What's
  the time?
**¿Qué pasa?** What's the
  matter?
**¡Qué pena!** It's a pity
**¿Qué tal?** How do you
  do? How are you?
**quedarse** remain, stay
**queja** f complaint
**quejarse** complain
**quemadura de sol**
  sunburn
**quemar** burn
**querer** want
**querido/a** dear
**queso** m cheese
**¿Quién?** Who?
**quieto** still (quiet)
**quincena** f fortnight
**quiosko** m kiosk, news
  stand
**quiste** m cyst

**quitaesmalte** nail polish
  remover
**quizás** maybe, perhaps

## R

**rábano** m radish
**rabia** f rabies
**radiador** m radiator
**radio** f radio
**radiografía** f X-ray
**rallado/a** grated
**rana** f frog
**rancio/a** stale
**rápidamente** quickly
**rápido/a** fast
**raqueta** f racket
**raqueta de tenis**
  tennis racket
**raro/a** foreign, strange,
  odd, rare, weird
**rascar** scratch (vb)
**rasgado** torn
**rastrillo** m rake
**rata** f rat
**ratero/a** m/f
  pickpocket
**ratón** m mouse
**rayado/a** striped
**rayo** m lightning, spoke
  (of wheel)
**raza** f race (people)
**razonable** reasonable
**real** real, royal
**realmente** really
**rebajas** fpl sale
**rebanada** f slice
**rebeca** f cardigan
**recado** m message

SPANISH → ENGLISH

**recalentar** overheat
**recargar** recharge
**recaudador/a** m/f
  receiver (tax)
**recepción** f reception
**recepcionista** m/f
  receptionist
**receta** f prescription,
  recipe
**rechazar** refuse (vb)
**recibo** m receipt
**recientemente**
  recently
**recogedor** m dustpan
**recoger** collect
**recolección de
  equipajes** baggage
  reclaim
**recomendar**
  recommend
**reconocer** recognize
**recordar** remember
**recuerdo** m souvenir
**red** f net, web
**redondo/a** round
**reducción** f reduction
**reducir** reduce
**reembolsar** refund (vb)
**reembolso** m
  refund (n)
**reemplazo de cadera**
  hip replacement
**refractario/a**
  ovenproof
**refresco** m soft drink
**refrigerador** m fridge
**regalar** present (vb)

**regalo** m gift,
  present (n)
**regalo de boda**
  wedding present
**regalo de
  cumpleaños**
  birthday present
**región** f region
**registrar** check, inspect
**registrarse** check in
**registro** m register (n)
**regla** f ruler
**regresar** come back,
  return
**reina** f queen
**Reino Unido** United
  Kingdom
**reír** laugh (vb)
**relámpago** flash (of
  lightning)
**relleno/a** stuffed
**relleno** m filling
  (sandwich)
**reloj** m clock, watch
**remar** row (vb)
**remendar** mend
**remo** m oar
**remolcar** tow
**remolque** m caravan,
  trailer
**reparación** f repair (n)
**reparar** fix, repair (vb)
**repelente de insectos**
  insect repellent
**repetir** repeat
**repleto/a** crowded
**repollo** m cabbage

**representación** f performance

**representante de ventas** sales representative

**República Checa** Czech Republic

**República de Eslovaquia** Slovak Republic

**requerir** require

**resaca** f hangover

**resbaladizo/a** slippery

**resbalarse** slip

**rescate** m rescue (n)

**rescate de montaña** mountain rescue

**reserva** f reservation

**reserva natural** nature reserve

**reservar** reserve

**residente** m/f resident (adj, n)

**residuo** m waste

**resistente al horno** ovenproof

**respetuoso/a** polite

**respirar** breathe

**responder** answer (vb)

**respuesta** f answer, reply (n)

**resto** m rest (remainder)

**retirado/a** retired

**retrato** m portrait

**reuma** m rheumatism

**reunión** f meeting

**revelación** f exposure

**revelado** film processing

**revés** m reverse (n)

**revisor/a** m/f ticket collector

**revista** f magazine

**rey** m king

**rezar** pray

**rico/a** delicious, rich

**ridículo/a** ridiculous

**rímel** m mascara

**riña** f quarrel (n)

**riñón** m kidney

**río** m river

**risa** f laugh (n)

**rizado/a** curly

**robado** mugged, stolen

**robar** steal

**roble** m oak

**robo** m break-in, burglary, theft

**roca** f rock

**rodeado** surrounded

**rodilla** f knee

**rojo/a** red

**rollo** m coil (n, rope)

**romper** break

**ron** m rum

**roncar** snore

**ropa** f clothing, gear

**ropa de cama** bed linen

**ropa de hombre** menswear

**ropa de mujer** ladies' wear

**ropa interior** lingerie, underpants, underwear

SPANISH → ENGLISH

SPANISH → ENGLISH

**ropas** fpl  clothes
**ropero** m  cupboard
**rosa** f  rose (flower)
**rosa** m  pink
**rosquilla** f  doughnut
**roto/a**  broken
**rotonda** f  roundabout
**rubeola** f  German measles, rubella
**rubio/a**  fair (hair colour)
**rueda** f  wheel
**ruido** m  noise
**ruidoso/a**  loud, noisy
**ruina** f  ruin

## S

**sábado** m  Saturday
**sábana** f  sheet
**saber**  know
**sabor** m  flavour
**sacacorcho** m  corkscrew
**saco de dormir**  sleeping bag
**sagrado/a**  holy
**sal** f  salt
**sala** f  hall, ward (hospital)
**sala de embarque**  departure lounge
**sala de espera**  waiting room
**sala de estar**  living room, lounge
**sala municipal**  town hall
**salado/a**  savoury
**salario** m  wage

**salchicha** f  sausage
**salida** f  departure, exit
**salida de emergencia**  emergency exit, fire exit
**salir**  depart, leave
**salmón** m  salmon
**salmón ahumado**  smoked salmon
**salón** m  lounge
**salón de belleza**  beauty salon
**salsa** f  gravy, sauce
**saltar**  jump (vb)
**salto** m  jump (n)
**salto de esquí**  ski jump
**¡Salud!**  Cheers!
**saludable**  healthy
**saludo** m  greeting
**salvar**  rescue (vb)
**sandalia** f  sandal
**sandía** f  watermelon
**sandwich** m  sandwich
**sangrar**  bleed
**sangre** f  blood
**sapo** m  toad
**sarampión** m  measles
**sartén** f  frying pan
**sastre** m  tailor
**se puede romper**  breakable
**secador de pelo**  hairdryer
**secadora** f  dryer, spin-dryer
**secar**  blow-dry
**sección** f  department
**seco/a**  dry

184

**secretario/a** m/f
secretary

**seda** f silk

**seguir** follow

**segunda clase**
second-class

**segunda mano**
second-hand

**segundo/a** second

**seguro** m insurance

**seguro contra
terceros** third-party
insurance

**seguro de coche** car
insurance

**seguro de vida** life
insurance

**seguro médico**
medical insurance

**seguro/a** safe (adj),
sure

**sello** m stamp, postage
stamp

**semáforo** m traffic light

**semana** f week

**semana pasada** last
week

**semana próxima** next
week

**Semana Santa** Easter

**semanalmente** weekly

**sencillo/a** simple

**sendero** m path,
footpath

**sendero de bicicletas**
cycle track

**sentarse** sit

**sentencia** f sentence
(law)

**sentir** feel

**señal** f signal

**señal de marcar**
dialling tone

**señal de tráfico** road
sign

**señalar** point (vb)

**señor** m Mr

**señora** f Mrs, lady

**señorita** f Miss, Ms

**separado/a** separate

**séptico/a** septic

**septiembre** m
September

**ser** be

**serio/a** serious

**serpiente** f snake

**servicio** m service

**servicio de caballeros**
gents' toilet

**servicio de courier/
entrega** courier
service

**servicio de damas**
ladies' toilet

**servicios** mpl bath-
room, cloakroom,
lavatory, toilet

**servilleta** f napkin,
serviette

**servilletas de papel**
paper napkins/serviettes

**servir** pour

**sexo** m sex

**si** if

**sí** yes

SPANISH → ENGLISH

185

SPANISH → ENGLISH

**si no** otherwise, if not
**sidra f** cider
**siempre** always
**siga derecho** straight on
**siglo m** century
**significar** mean, intend
**silencio m** silence
**silla f** chair
**silla alta** high chair
**silla de montar** saddle
**silla de patio** deck chair
**silla de ruedas** pushchair, wheelchair
**sillón m** armchair
**simpático/a** friendly
**simple** plain
**simular** fake (vb)
**sin** without
**sin alcohol** non-alcoholic
**sin camiseta** topless
**sin plomo** lead-free
**sinagoga f** synagogue
**sobre** above, on, over
**sobre m** envelope
**sobrina f** niece
**sobrino m** nephew
**sobrio/a** sober
**socio/a m/f** partner (business)
**socorrista m/f** lifeguard
**soda f** soda
**sofá m** couch
**soga f** rope
**sol m** sun

**solamente** just, only
**soleado/a** sunny
**solicitud f** request (n)
**solo** alone, single
**sólo** only (adv)
**soltero/a** single
**soluble** soluble
**sombra f** shade
**sombra de ojos** eye shadow
**sombrero m** hat
**sombrilla f** sunshade
**somnífero m** sleeping pill
**son** are
**sonar** ring (vb)
**sonreír** smile (vb)
**sopa f** soup
**sordo/a** deaf
**sostén m** bra
**sótano m** basement
**su** her, his
**suave** soft
**subir** climb, get on
**submarinismo m** scuba diving
**subterráneo m** tunnel
**subterráneo/a** underground (adj)
**subtítulo m** subtitle
**sucio/a** dirty, nasty
**sucursal f** branch (office)
**Sudáfrica** South Africa
**sudafricano/a** South African (adj, n)
**sudar** sweat (vb)
**Suecia f** Sweden

**sueco/a** m/f Swedish, Swede (adj, n)
**suegra** f mother-in-law
**suegro** m father-in-law
**suegros** mpl in-laws, parents-in-law
**suela** f sole (shoe)
**sueldo** m wage
**suelo** m floor (of room)
**suelto/a** loose
**suerte** f luck
**suéter** m jumper, sweater
**suficiente** plenty, enough
**Suiza** Switzerland
**suizo/a** m/f Swiss (adj, n)
**suizo-alemán** Swiss-German
**superior** up-market
**suplemento** m supplement
**sur** m south
**suspensión** f suspension

**T**
**tabla de planchar** ironing board
**tabla de surfear** surfboard
**tablilla** f shingle
**tablón de anuncios** noticeboard
**tal vez** maybe, perhaps
**taladro** m drill (n)
**talco** m talcum powder

**talla media** medium sized
**talón** m heel
**tamaño** m size
**también** also, too
**tampón** m tampon
**tanque** m tank
**tanque séptico** septic tank
**tapa** f lid
**tapado** jammed
**tapón** m plug (bath)
**tarde** late
**tarde** f afternoon, early evening
**tarea** f housework
**tarifa** f fare
**tarjeta** f card
**tarjeta de crédito** charge card, credit card
**tarjeta de cumpleaños** birthday card
**tarjeta de embarque** boarding card
**tarjeta de identidad** identity card
**tarjeta de identidad bancario** cheque card
**tarjeta de llamadas** phone card
**tarta** f cake
**taxi** m cab, taxi
**taxista** m/f taxi driver
**taza** f cup
**tazón** m mug
**té** m tea

SPANISH → ENGLISH

**té de hierbas, té natural** herbal tea
**teatro** m theatre
**techo** m roof
**techo corredizo** sunroof
**tejer** knit
**tejido** m knitwear, material, fabric
**teleférico** m cable car
**teléfono** m phone, telephone
**teléfono móvil** mobile phone
**teléfono pago/público** payphone
**televisión** f television
**temperatura** f temperature
**templo** m temple
**temporada** f season
**temporario** temporary
**tendedero** m clothes line
**tendón** m tendon
**tenedor** m fork
**tener** have, hold
**tener miedo** be afraid of
**tener que** have to
**tener sed** thirsty
**tener suerte** lucky
**tengo dolor** it's sore
**tenis** m tennis
**tentempié** m snack
**teñir** dye (vb)
**termas** fpl hot spring
**terminal** m terminal

**terminar** finish (vb)
**termo** m flask
**termómetro** m thermometer
**ternera** f calf, veal
**terremoto** m earthquake
**terrible** awful
**terrón** m lump
**testigo** m/f witness
**teta** f breast
**tetera** f teapot
**tetina** f teat (bottle)
**tía** f aunt
**tiempo** m weather
**tienda** f shop, store, food shop
**tienda de alimentos naturales** health food shop
**tienda de departamentos** department store
**tierra** f earth, ground, land
**tijeras** fpl scissors
**tijeras para uñas** nail scissors
**timbre** m doorbell
**tímido/a** shy
**timón** m rudder
**tinta** f ink
**tinte** m dye (n)
**tintorería** f dry cleaner's
**tío** m uncle
**típico/a** typical
**tipo** m sort, type

**tipo de cambio** rate
  of exchange
**tirante** tight
**tirar** pull
**tisú** m tissue
**título** degree
  (qualification)
**toalla** f towel
**tobillo** m ankle
**toca discos** CD player
**tocino** m bacon
**todavía** still (yet)
**todo** everything
**todo** m whole (n)
**todo junto** altogether
**todos/todas** m/f
  everyone
**tomar** take
**tomar prestado**
  borrow
**tomate** m tomato
**tonto/a** silly
**torcedura** f sprain (n)
**torcer** sprain (vb)
**tormenta** f storm,
  thunderstorm
**tornillo** m nut (for bolt),
  screw
**torre** f tower
**tortilla** f omelette
**tos** f cough (n)
**toser** cough (vb)
**total** m total
**totalmente** completely
**trabajar** work
**trabajar por cuenta
  propia** self-employed
**trabajo** m job

**trabajo doméstico**
  housework
**traducción** f translation
**traducir** translate
**traductor/a** m/f
  translator
**traer** bring, fetch
**tráfico** m traffic
**tragar** swallow (vb)
**traje** m suit
**traje de agua** wetsuit
**traje de baño/
  bañador** swimming
  costume
**trampolín** m diving
  board
**tranquilo/a** quiet
**transbordador** m ferry
**transbordador de
  coches** car ferry
**transpiración** f
  sweat (n)
**tranvía** m tram
**trapo** m duster, rag,
  floorcloth
**trapo de cocina**
  dishtowel
**trato** m deal
**travesía** f journey
**tren** m train
**trenza** f plait
**trineo** m sledge
**triste** sad
**trotar** jog (vb)
**trote** m jog (n)
**trozo** m lump
**trucha** f trout
**trueno** m thunder

**SPANISH → ENGLISH**

**tú** you
**tu** your
**tubo** m tube
**tubo de escape**
  exhaust pipe
**tubo de respiración**
  snorkel
**tubo interno** inner tube
**tumbona** f deck chair
**túnel** m tunnel
**turco/a** m/f Turkish,
  Turk (adj, n)
**turismo** m
  sightseeing
**turquesa** f turquoise
**Turquía** Turkey

## U

**úlcera** f ulcer
**úlcera de boca** mouth
  ulcer
**último/a** last
**un poco** bit
**una vez** once
**uniforme** even (adj)
**Unión Europea** EU
**unirse** join
**universidad** f
  university
**uno** m one
**unos/unas** some
**uña** f nail
**urgencias** casualty
  department
**urgente** urgent
**usar** use, wear
**utensilios de cocina**
  cooking utensils

**útil** useful
**uvas** fpl grapes

## V

**vaca** f cow
**vacaciones** fpl
  vacation, holidays
**vacaciones
  organizadas**
  package holiday
**vacío/a** empty
**vacuna** f vaccine
**vago/a** lazy
**vagón** m carriage
**vainilla** f vanilla
**¡Vale!** OK!
**vale** all right
**vale** m voucher
**válido/a** valid
**valle** m valley
**valor** m value
**válvula** f valve
**vapor** m steam
**varicela** f chicken pox
**varios/as** several
**vaso** m glass (tumbler)
**vasto/a** great
**vecino/a** m/f neighbour
**vegetales** mpl
  vegetables
**vegetariano/a** m/f
  vegetarian
**vehículo** m vehicle
**vela** f candle
**velocidad** f speed
**velocímetro** m
  speedometer
**vena** f vein

**vencer** expire
**venda** f bandage
**vendaje** m dressing, bandage
**vendedor/a** m/f salesperson
**vender** sell
**veneno** m poison
**venenoso/a** poisonous
**venir** come
**ventana** f window
**ventilador** m fan
**ventoso/a** windy
**ver** see
**verano** m summer
**verdadero/a** true
**verde** green
**verdulería** greengrocer's
**verduras** fpl vegetables
**verduras orgánicas** organic vegetables
**vereda** f sidewalk
**vergüenza** f shame
**vestíbulo** m lobby
**vestido** m dress
**vestido de noche** nightdress
**vestuario** m changing room
**veterinario/a** m/f vet, veterinarian
**vía** via
**viajar** travel
**viaje** m journey, tour
**viaje de negocios** business trip

**viaje en barco** boat trip
**vida** f life
**vidriera** f shop window
**viejo/a** ancient, old
**Viena** Vienna
**viento** m wind
**viernes** m Friday
**Viernes Santo** Good Friday
**vinagre** m vinegar
**vinagreta** f salad dressing
**vino** m wine
**vino de la casa** house wine
**vino de mesa** table wine
**vino medio seco** medium dry wine
**vino tinto** red wine
**viñedo** m vineyard
**violación** f rape (n)
**violar** rape (vb)
**violeta** f violet (adj, n)
**virus** m virus
**visa** f visa
**visita guiada** guided tour
**visitante** m/f visitor
**visitar** visit
**vista** f sight, view
**vitrina** f shop window
**viudo/a** m/f widower, widow
**vivero** m nursery (plants)
**vivir** live

**SPANISH → ENGLISH**

**vivo/a** lively
**volante** m steering wheel
**volar** fly (vb)
**volcán** m volcano
**voltaje** m voltage
**volver** go back, return, turn, come back
**vomitar** vomit
**¡Voy a vomitar!** I'm going to be sick!
**voz** f voice
**vuelo** m flight
**vuelo chárter** charter flight
**vuelo de conexión** connecting flight
**vuelo libre** hang-gliding

## Y

**y** and
**ya** already
**yate** m yacht
**yema** f yolk
**yerno** m son-in-law
**yeso** m plaster
**yo** I
**yo estoy** I am
**yo mismo** myself
**yo soy** I am

## Z

**zanahoria** f carrot
**zapatillas** fpl slippers
**zapato** m shoe
**zona** f zone
**zorro/a** m/f fox
**zumo** m juice
**zumo de fruta** fruit juice
**zumo de naranja** orange juice
**zurdo/a** left-handed